LANGUAGE AN

Dorothy S. Stric
Celia Genishi and Donn
ADVISORY BOARD: *Richard Allington,*
Anne Haas Dyson, Carole Edelsky, Mary Ju.

MW00574708

continued

Reading and Representing Across the Content Areas
AMY ALEXANDRA WILSON & KATHRYN J. CHAVEZ

Writing and Teaching to Change the World
STEPHANIE JONES, ED.

Educating Literacy Teachers Online
LANE W. CLARKE & SUSAN WATTS-TAFFEE

Other People's English
VERSHAWN ASHANTI YOUNG ET AL.

WHAM! Teaching with Graphic Novels Across
the Curriculum
WILLIAM G. BROZO, GARY MOORMAN, & CARLA K. MEYER

The Administration and Supervision of Reading Programs,
5th Ed.
SHELLEY B. WEPNER ET AL., EDS.

Critical Literacy in the Early Childhood Classroom
CANDACE R. KUBY

Inspiring Dialogue
MARY M. JUZWIK ET AL.

Reading the Visual
FRANK SERAFINI

Race, Community, and Urban Schools
STUART GREENE

ReWRITING the Basics
ANNE HAAS DYSON

Writing Instruction That Works
ARTHUR N. APPLEBEE ET AL.

Literacy Playshop
KAREN E. WOHLWEND

Critical Media Pedagogy
ERNEST MORRELL ET AL.

A Search Past Silence
DAVID E. KIRKLAND

The ELL Writer
CHRISTINA ORTMEIER-HOOPER

Reading in a Participatory Culture
HENRY JENKINS ET AL., EDS.

Real World Writing for Secondary Students
JESSICA SINGER EARLY & MEREDITH DECOSTA

Teaching Vocabulary to English Language Learners
MICHAEL F. GRAVES ET AL.

Literacy for a Better World
LAURA SCHNEIDER VANDERPLOEG

Socially Responsible Literacy
PAULA M. SELVESTER & DEBORAH G. SUMMERS

Learning from Culturally and Linguistically Diverse
Classrooms
JOAN C. FINGON & SHARON H. ULANOFF, EDS.

Bridging Literacy and Equity
ALTHIER M. LAZAR ET AL.

"Trust Me! I Can Read"
SALLY LAMPING & DEAN WOODRING BLASE

Reading Girls
HADAR DUBROWSKY MA'AYAN

Reading Time
CATHERINE COMPTON-LILLY

A Call to Creativity
LUKE REYNOLDS

Literacy and Justice Through Photography
WENDY EWALD ET AL.

The Successful High School Writing Center
DAWN FELS & JENNIFER WELLS, EDS.

Interrupting Hate
MOLLIE V. BLACKBURN

Playing Their Way into Literacies
KAREN E. WOHLWEND

Teaching Literacy for Love and Wisdom
JEFFREY D. WILHELM & BRUCE NOVAK

Overtested
JESSICA ZACHER PANDYA

Restructuring Schools for Linguistic Diversity, 2nd Ed.
OFELIA B. MIRAMONTES ET AL.

Words Were All We Had
MARÍA DE LA LUZ REYES, ED.

Urban Literacies
VALERIE KINLOCH, ED.

Bedtime Stories and Book Reports
CATHERINE COMPTON-LILLY & STUART GREENE, EDS.

Envisioning Knowledge
JUDITH A. LANGER

Envisioning Literature, 2nd Ed.
JUDITH A. LANGER

Writing Assessment and the Revolution in Digital Texts
and Technologies
MICHAEL R. NEAL

Artifactual Literacies
KATE PAHL & JENNIFER ROWSELL

(Re)Imagining Content-Area Literacy Instruction
RONI JO DRAPER, ED.

Change Is Gonna Come
PATRICIA A. EDWARDS ET AL.

When Commas Meet Kryptonite
MICHAEL BITZ

Literacy Tools in the Classroom
RICHARD BEACH ET AL.

Harlem on Our Minds
VALERIE KINLOCH

Teaching the New Writing
ANNE HERRINGTON ET AL., EDS.

Children, Language, and Literacy
CELIA GENISHI & ANNE HAAS DYSON

Children's Language
JUDITH WELLS LINDFORS

Children's Literature and Learning
BARBARA A. LEHMAN

Storytime
LAWRENCE R. SIPE

The Effective Literacy Coach
ADRIAN RODGERS & EMILY M. RODGERS

Reading the Media
RENEE HOBBS

What Was It Like?
LINDA J. RICE

Research on Composition
PETER SMAGORINSKY, ED.

New Literacies in Action
WILLIAM KIST

Translanguaging for Emergent Bilinguals

Inclusive Teaching in the Linguistically Diverse Classroom

Danling Fu | Xenia Hadjioannou | Xiaodi Zhou

Foreword by Ofelia García

TEACHERS COLLEGE PRESS

TEACHERS COLLEGE | COLUMBIA UNIVERSITY

NEW YORK AND LONDON

Published by Teachers College Press, 1234 Amsterdam Avenue, New York, NY 10027

Library of Congress Cataloging-in-Publication Data is available at loc.gov

Names: Fu, Danling, author. | Hadjioannou, Xenia, author. | Zhou, Xiaodi, author.
Title: Translanguaging for emergent bilinguals : inclusive teaching in the linguistically diverse classroom / Danling Fu, Xenia Hadjioannou, Xiaodi Zhou.
Description: First edition. | New York : Teachers College Press, [2019] | Series: Language and literacy series | Includes bibliographical references and index.
Identifiers: LCCN 2018050301|
ISBN   9780807761137 (hardcover : alk. paper)
ISBN   9780807761120 (pbk. : alk. paper)
Subjects: LCSH: Education, Bilingual. | Translanguaging (Linguistics)
Classification: LCC LC3715 .F8 2019 | DDC 370.117—dc23
LC record available at https://lccn.loc.gov/2018050301

ISBN 978-0-8077-6112-0 (paper)
ISBN 978-0-8077-6113-7 (hardcover)
ISBN 978-0-8077-7757-2 (ebook)

Printed on acid-free paper
Manufactured in the United States of America

Dedications

Danling – For my family, especially the new addition, Allie, hope that she will be able to enjoy the multilingual world with pride and competence

Xenia – For my family of inveterate translanguagers, and mostly for Erik

Xiaodi – For my family, particularly Alexandra, and for those students in our classrooms who cross languages and cultures daily

Contents

Foreword
Breathing Life into a Translanguaging Room

In an era of punitive accountability and racializing discourses where all but White "native-born" Americans are criminals, this book offers an uplifting alternative view of the lives and education of language-minoritized students. Fu, Hadjioannou, and Zhou present here a practice-based approach to translanguaging for all types of teachers of emergent bilinguals. We are invited into what the authors call a multifunctional translanguaging room. There, they tell us, "You have access to all language features and tools in your repertoire and can flexibly select and use what you need at any given moment. You may not use every single thing in the room simultaneously, but it is all there within reach." This is exactly what the authors do in this book, put all the translanguaging understandings *within reach of all teachers,* all integrated in a single room and within reach of all.

This book does more than design the translanguaging room—it populates this room with students of all types and their teachers. There are students who speak Spanish, but also Arabic, Chinese, Dyula, French, Haitian Creole, Urdu, Vietnamese. Students are portrayed as active learners in classrooms of language arts, math, science, social studies. And they are in different school programs—ESL programs, transitional bilingual education, dual language bilingual education, and mainstream classrooms. There are no simple descriptions of translanguaging pedagogical tools in this book; there are teachers and students *using* the tools for different purposes to meet the academic, social, and institutional challenges that emergent bilingual students face.

With remarkable writing ability, the authors in this book breathe life into a multifunctional translanguaging room through the vignettes in each chapter. For example, after meeting Rosa, a 4th-grader in an ESL pull-out program, and discussing the challenges that she faces in an instructional program that doesn't meet her needs, the authors introduce Yan, a student who is also in an ESL program but in what might be considered a translanguaging classroom. The translanguaging pedagogical practices are not simply described; they are felt "in the flesh," as Yan learns content while developing English, and uses all his language resources to learn collaboratively with his teacher and peers, whereas Rosa lingers in frustration in her ESL traditional classroom.

The students in the vignettes are not simple cutouts— they move, they grow, they develop. For example, we see Yan in the fall, but also as he interacts differently in the spring. This sense of action-in-time is felt throughout the book. We first meet Maria, a United States–born emergent bilingual, as a 4th-grader. But we also see her act as a 7th-grader 3 years later. And Jingming is introduced not as a student in the transitional bilingual program in which he was placed when he first arrived, but as an alumnus of such a program. We are made to feel Jingming's pain, for his success in becoming literate in English comes at the price of his inability to read Chinese. The authors do not shy away from the socioemotional challenges that emergent bilingual students face as walls are erected that partition their identities and confine them to a specific room.

The book focuses on students and teachers in schools, but the initial vignette is about a teleconference between multinational professionals. The authors' own multilingual lives, as well as that of one of their children, figure prominently here. This is because the goal of the translanguaging teaching transformation that the authors propose goes beyond simply touching students' lives. The purpose of designing a room that brings all aspects of emergent bilingual lives together is precisely to enable them to break away from the structural constraints that are placed in their lives as language-minoritized and racialized people. Translanguaging pedagogical practice is presented as having the potential to develop critical bilingual readers and writers, who are able to decry the raciolinguistic ideologies that have robbed them of their personhood and to work on the structural changes needed for social justice.

This is a book that is deeply critical of educational practices that rob emergent bilinguals of educational and social opportunities. But the authors, experienced educators, offer a creative alternative, breathing life into the translanguaging space they construct through the action of students and teachers. In this multifunctional translanguaging room one can access the past, present, and future of students as well as different classrooms and programs, relating time–space in what the philosopher of language, Mikhail Bakhtin, called a "chronotope." In the multifunctional translanguaging room designed by the authors, we have access to different time–space configurations, and the potential to transform the racially charged, unjust social and educational practices of the present. It is all here, "within reach."

—Ofelia García, The Graduate Center, City University of New York

Acknowledgments

This book is inspired by Ofelia García's work, especially her conceptualization of *translanguaging* theories and practice. Her view on translanguaging not only raised the consciousness of our own multilingual transaction and our living experience as bilinguals, but also ignited us to revisit the studies we have done in the past years and reshaped our perspective and positions as literacy researchers and educators. We owe her a great deal for her role in shaping who we have become as language and literacy educators. Her foreword for our book has lifted us in the air!

Emily Spangler's initial invitation and many constructive suggestions, especially at the proposal stage, have enabled us to dig deeper in our thinking, write with strong focus, and reach a broad audience. We are deeply grateful for her knowledge, vigor, trust, and support. It has been a great pleasure to go through this journey under her editorial guidance.

We want to give our special thanks to our developmental editor, Susan Liddicoat, one of the best editors we have ever worked with. Her careful and thoughtful work enabled us to glide through the revision stage and end up with a stronger, more readable manuscript. Our thanks also go to our copy and production editors Jennifer Baker and Kathy Caveney: Their final review and suggestions to the manuscript have given our work a bright touch.

We truly appreciate our close friend and colleague, Nancy Shelton, for being by our side from the very beginning of writing this book, talking with us through ideas, encouraging us through roadblocks, and reading our manuscript with a sharp mind. Her hard questions on details often pushed us toward important insights and compelled us to reword and reposition our writing. We also need to thank several other colleagues and friends who, at different parts of the writing process, listened, asked for clarifications, and generously offered ideas, pushing our thinking and our writing forward.

Finally, we thank our families. Not only are they strong supporters of our work, but also give us beautiful and rich translanguaging living experiences, which are the foundation for this book.

Introduction

Bilinguals move through life using their languages to make sense of the world, to communicate with others, to express who they are. Sometimes they use one language, sometimes another. Other times they use language features from more than one language when they talk or write.

Importantly, regardless of the words coming out of their mouths or flowing from their pens or their cursors, when they engage with the world, they do so as bilinguals, with all their languages at the ready to partake in the experience. Yet, when emergent bilinguals arrive at our schools, we often lose sight of the fact that they are bilinguals in the making. We tell them to put aside all the language knowledge they already have beyond the language of instruction (i.e., English), and to single-mindedly focus their sense-making, their communication efforts, and their expression to that language alone. Shouldn't we instead be trying to help them reach their potential as accomplished bilinguals? Shouldn't we be encouraging them to use *all* their language knowledge to support their school learning? A translanguaging approach to the education of emergent bilinguals can offer auspicious routes to these alternative destinations. We begin this book by tracing our own journeys toward a translanguaging perspective and explain what translanguaging is and how it works in the lives of bilinguals. Following that, we turn our attention to school settings and use vignettes from the lives of emergent and expert bilinguals to explore the challenges they encounter in monolingually oriented classrooms and to offer promising alternatives through inclusive translanguaging classrooms.

All three of us authors are bilinguals or trilinguals. Danling Fu grew up speaking Chinese and learned English as a foreign language. Xenia Hadjioannou grew up speaking the Cypriot Greek dialect and Greek, and learned English as a foreign language. Xiaodi Zhou grew up speaking Chinese, learned English as a second language, and Spanish as a foreign language.

All three of us have been English teachers within and beyond U.S. borders. We learned and taught English from a monolingual perspective and rarely encouraged our students to use their first language to enhance their English learning. Now we are literacy educators and researchers. Danling has spent over a dozen years working in New York City schools with large numbers of students labeled English learners (ELs). Xenia has over the past 2 decades taught in pre- and inservice teacher education programs that prepare mainstream teachers to work with linguistically diverse students in their classrooms. After teaching English in the United States and China for many years, Xiaodi has recently completed his longitudinal study on bilingual and bicultural Mexican American youths living in new-immigrant, non-English-speaking families and communities in the southeastern region of the United States. All three of us are educators in language and literacy education with a special interest in researching and working with emergent bilingual students.

Our work has deepened and transformed our understanding of the literacy development of students who are learning English as an additional language, and we have moved away from a monolingual, language-separate perspective that regards students' home languages as irrelevant or even as potential obstacles to their proficiencies in English. Rather, we have come to develop a perspective that acknowledges all of students' languages as crucial contributors to their language and literacy development. In other words, we have adopted a *translanguaging* orientation to teaching and learning and, through a long and gradual journey, we now see English learners as emergent bilinguals (EBs) whose language proficiencies develop together as they grow and learn. Therefore, throughout the book, we use *emergent bilinguals* (EB) to refer to students who are learning English as an additional language and who, in U.S. public education, are typically referred to as English Learners (ELs). Readers will still encounter ELs whenever we are citing statistical and academic resources that use the term, or when referencing their designation as such in school settings. However, in our discussion and recommendations, we default to *emergent bilinguals*, a term that is more closely aligned to our theoretical perspective.

THE JOURNEY FROM A MONOLINGUAL TO A TRANSLANGUAGING PERSPECTIVE

How did our thinking about language learning change over the course of our experience as literacy educators? What in our personal and professional experiences moved us away from a monolingual perspective to adopting translanguaging? In what follows, we share Danling's journey to a translanguaging orientation to teaching and learning. We hope that this will help explain our position, but also challenge you to examine your own perspective of language learning.

I (Danling) learned and taught English as a foreign language in China for over 10 years before I came to the United States to pursue graduate studies. Throughout my English learning and teaching experiences in China, I had firmly believed that languages existed as separate entities in the minds of speakers. I thought that as people learned to speak their home language, that language would grow and occupy a specific spot in their minds. If they learned another language, then that developed separately, independently on its own. If anything, I feared that my own and my students' home languages interfered with our ability to become thoroughly proficient in English. In other words, I faithfully adopted a language-separate perspective. I still remember vividly one of my English teachers telling our class: "If you can dream in English, and forget your first language, you can say you have truly mastered English." In order to "truly master English," I tried very hard to forget Chinese and immerse myself in English. I forbade myself to touch Chinese books so I could focus on learning English during my college years. I memorized every text we read, and took every opportunity to read, write, and listen to English as much as I could. When I became an English teacher, I required my students to do the same. But after a decade of learning English this way, I still never managed to dream in English. My quest to perfect my English led me to decide to continue my studies in an English-speaking country, with a determination to speak, write, and think like English-speaking natives by totally immersing myself in an English-speaking environment.

I started my new life in the United States in a small New England town that had only a few Chinese residents, and I began my graduate studies in a small college with just a few Asian faces. Not only was I homesick for my family and Chinese food, but I missed speaking Chinese tremendously. I remember one day when I saw a Korean boy in the hallway at school, Chinese jumped off my tongue as I excitedly greeted him. It was not until a few sentences later, when his confused smile sank in, that I realized he had no idea what I was saying. This incident made me realize that Chinese was an integral part of me. Ironically, after all my efforts to cut myself off from Chinese while learning English, when I began my life in an English-dominant environment, I would get excited and joyful to see other Chinese people, and chatting with them in Chinese would give me a sense of ease, intimacy, and comfort. Every night before I went to bed, I would read a few pages of Chinese books or newspapers, a reward I gave myself as a favorite dessert after a hard day of an English-only reading and writing diet.

After a few years of immersion in an English environment, English did finally enter my dreams, but never alone or in a pure English-speaking setting. I remember I once had a dream that I was on a bus, but it was not like in the United States or China, and I was speaking a mixture of both English and Chinese with the people around me. I was so puzzled by this strange dream that I told my friends about it, and continued to think about it for a long time. Despite the comingling of English and Chinese in my dreams, I still faithfully followed an unmixed Chinese or English policy in my studies and teaching. I rarely allowed myself to mix both languages, though I often had to use my native language to think through a new concept I learned in English or to articulate an appropriate expression in my English writing.

My professional training in the United States is in literacy education, which has expanded into the second language and bilingual field through my research and work in schools with a focus on the literacy development of new immigrant students. First, through my study on Laotian refugee youths,

I came to understand that when teaching students with interrupted formal education (SIFE), we should not single-mindedly focus on grade-level curriculum but start from where they are, wherever that might be, and work to move with them to their next level (Fu, 1995). Teaching students, rather than adhering to curriculum or standards, was the big takeaway from my research with refugee adolescents. Then I spent over a dozen years working as a literacy consultant, first in California and later in New York City, in schools where the majority of students were new immigrants.

In the late 1990s, I began working as a consultant in a middle school in New York City's Chinatown, where 90% of students were Chinese immigrants. The administrators and teachers lamented the slow development of their students' English proficiency. They said that even after 3–4 years of studying in this school, many students still couldn't speak much English because they spoke Chinese most of time—in the school with their peers, as well as at home and out in the Chinatown community. Ultimately, the lack of oral English proficiency hindered students' overall English literacy development. They were considered "long-term" ELs, and were consistently placed in the bilingual program, which was mostly intended for beginning English learners. Both parents and students were bothered by this "beginner-level" stigma that hung over them for years. When I saw that the lack of practice with English was one of the main reasons for these students' slow English literacy development, per my own prior teaching experiences in China, I recommended an "English-only" policy: Push students to use as much English as possible. Based on my advice, only English was used in classrooms, and students were to be tasked with listening to English for homework: listen to books on tape and watch half an hour of news in English daily. When I made my regular visit to the school the following month, the teachers complained to me that "English-only" didn't work in their classrooms. "Now students have become very silent," they said. "In the past, at least they spoke Chinese in their group discussion; now they don't speak." I realized I had made a mistake.

By working closely with EB students and their teachers and after reading Jim Cummins's (1979) theory of language interdependence, I gained an understanding of the importance of students' home language in their second language literacy development. It became obvious to me that students' home languages play an important role in their overall literacy development and, as a result, they need to be given purposeful and legitimate spaces in the classroom. In my book *An Island of English* (Fu, 2003), I addressed the important role of EB students' home language in their English literacy development and advocated not only for curriculum integration, but also language integration in bilingual and English as a second language (ESL) programs. My recommendation was to allow students' home language use in ESL and mainstream classrooms (usually considered an English-only program), and to encourage teachers in bilingual classrooms (usually considered a home-language-only program) to teach content-related English vocabulary and allow their students to read and write in English. The purpose of this integration was to maximize students' learning opportunities and thus the ESL and bilingual programs worked together to enhance students' content knowledge and English language development. The integration proved to be successful and enabled students to make significant progress in their overall academic achievement through frequently reading and writing in a mixture of both Chinese and English.

After closely examining volumes of emergent bilingual students' writing, in my book *Writing Between Languages* (Fu, 2009), I presented four stages of their writing development: from home language, to mixed language, to interlanguage, to finally reaching English proficiency. When describing the English writing development of EBs, I gave value not only to students' home language, but also emphasized their mixed language or code-switching and interlanguage practices as necessary stages in their writing development. Even with this recognition, however, the developmental trajectory I described clearly implies a unidirectional movement: toward English proficiency. But I concluded this book with a chapter on "Becoming Bilingual Writers," in which I wrote the following:

> Learning to write in English for ELLs who are literate in their native language is actually a process of becoming bilingual writers, rather than merely replacing one language or writing ability with another or mastering two separate language systems. ELLs' native language will always be part of them, their identity, their funds of knowledge, and their tools for thinking and expressing. (p. 120)

I now realize that by the end of writing this book, I had begun to drift away from my own conceptualization of a four-stage writing development for ELs or emergent bilinguals, and started to question the one-way movement from one stage to the other, ultimately leading learners to becoming English writers rather than bilingual ones. Three years later, when Marylou Matoush and I worked on our book *Focus on Literacy* (Fu & Matoush, 2014), we took a *languaging-as-thinking stance*, which we defined as "doing language, literacy and learning while being and becoming." We further illustrated this action:

> Language/literacy is pushing, provoking, generating, shaping, reshaping, transforming and connecting one's thinking (as well as one's preformed identity according to the situation), and at the same time, thinking is pushing, provoking, generating, shaping, reshaping, transforming and connecting one's language/literacy. (p. 14)

In this explanation we tried hard to present language as a verb, inseparable from thinking. In the book, we also stressed cross-language instruction and suggested encouraging students to use every possible resource available (including their home languages) to help them maximize their learning.

I first read about translanguaging in *Bilingual Education in the 21st Century* (García, 2009). Beyond a comprehensive discussion of program types, policies, and practices of bilingual education, García also includes a discussion of translanguaging, a concept that provides an alternative perspective to what it means to be a bilingual person, and suggests pedagogical implications for the education of emergent bilinguals. García argues that the cross-linguistic lens, which recognizes the potential influence of a previously learned language on the acquisition of a new language, does not fully capture the experience of bilinguals. Instead, she proposes a much more organic and interconnected relationship among all the languages bilinguals know. García suggests that at any given point, bilinguals translanguage by simultaneously using linguistic tools, knowledge, and features from all their languages. Indeed, García argues that even though linguistic analyses, grammar books, and language policies define, describe, and categorize languages and language varieties as distinct and separate from one another, these firm borders do not hold up in bilingual practice. Rather, bilinguals intermingle linguistic features from all their languages in ways that serve their communication needs. Translanguaging is thus "the communicative norm of bilingual communities and cannot be compared to a prescribed monolingual use" (p. 51).

García and Li (2014) more fully discuss translanguaging theory and practice in their book *Translanguaging: Language, Bilingualism and Education*, in which they adopt the idea that bilinguals are not "two monolinguals in one person" (Grosjean, 1989, p. 3) with distinct language repertoires for each of the languages they know. Rather, they posit that bilinguals have a single language repertoire that gives them more tools, richer resources, and more flexible ways to learn new knowledge, express themselves, and communicate with others.

In explaining translanguaging from the perspective of the ideal of a single linguistic repertoire, García and Li (2014) propose a reframing of the notions of "bilingualism" and "multilingualism." Customarily, when we think of bilinguals, we are thinking of people who either first knew one language and then learned a second one, or of people who grew up learning two different languages at the same time. This perception typically involves a conceptualization of adding one linguistic system next to another (or even more in the case of multilingualism). We may believe that this additive process involves some sort of interaction among these languages (Cummins's idea of language interdependence, [1979]), but in essence, we understand them as quintessentially separate linguistic systems. Indeed, even the prefixes *bi-* and *multi-* imply a collection of discrete items that can be readily numbered and counted.

García and Li (2014) propose expanding bilingualism toward a more dynamic conceptualization that assumes a single linguistic system and acknowledges that speakers have a very active decision-making role. Others propose the notion of "plurilingualism," which suggests a more fluid sense of plurality that matches better the idea of a single linguistic repertoire that encompasses all the language knowledge of an individual (e.g., Grosjean, 2010; Hornberger, 2003). Notably, the conceptual shift from multiple autonomous linguistic repertoires to a single integrated one is also important for instructional practice, as it recognizes that the development of proficiency in one language cannot reasonably be separated from the other languages and language tools of a speaker.

García and Li's (2014) conceptualization of translanguaging was both enlightening and intriguing as it provided a compelling, well-fitting framework for my evolving understandings of emergent bilinguals' language and literacy development, which had come a long way since my days of trying to forget my Chinese so I could truly master English. Translanguaging provides a welcome theoretical relief from monolingual perspectives that are singularly focused on acquisition of the target language. Translanguaging not only theorizes and names the natural communicative practice of bilinguals and multilinguals (bi/multilinguals), but also challenges the monolingual notions underlying the policies, curricula, and practice of current second language, foreign language, and bilingual programs across the world. It even goes beyond the concepts of language interdependence, code-switching practice, and linguistic hybridization, which, though giving value to all the languages of bi/multilinguals, are still grounded in a monolingual perspective: seeing languages as separate entities in a bilingual's brain. Translanguaging is rapidly gaining significant traction in language acquisition, literacy, and TESOL (Teaching English to speakers of other languages) circles. Notably, out of the 2,683 library search results we found for "translanguaging," 2,318 of the texts were published within the past 5 years. Equally noteworthy is the fact that beginning in 2013, translanguaging has seen an ever-increasing presence in practitioner-oriented publications and newsletters from TESOL and the National Council of Teachers of English (NCTE).

Learning about translanguaging prompted me to use this new lens to review my work of the past 2 decades on the literacy development of new immigrant students, which progressively addressed the significance of students' background knowledge, home language, and lived experience in their current school learning and English literacy development. Even though my work didn't associate with an "English-only" stance anymore, it was still grounded in a monolingual perspective, and described a unidirectional development of English learners or emergent bilinguals toward English proficiency, which ultimately would leave their home language by the wayside, weakened or completely forsaken.

Learning about translanguaging also made me reflect upon my own bilingual and bicultural experience. At home, I speak mostly English to my native English-speaking husband, and switch automatically to mostly Chinese, or mixed language when I speak to my son and my daughter-in-law, who are native Chinese speakers but are also proficient in English. When I chat with my Chinese students, we switch back and forth frequently between English and Chinese about their studies. In the past, I used to define this practice as code-switching. However, translanguaging helped me understand that even though we learn different languages with different features, once they are stored in our brains, these languages integrate into a new, single linguistic system, mixing and complementing like greens in a salad bowl. This new system of mixed languages, like a salad of mixed greens, functions together to benefit human lives and activities. If we fail to recognize this unified linguistic repertoire in bilinguals, we may privilege one language to the detriment of others or create artificial boundaries between them, rather than letting them work together synergistically to strengthen bilingual development as a whole system of becoming.

The concept of translanguaging also helps me understand myself as a Chinese American, which is my integrated identity. It is hard to say how much of me is Chinese and how much is American, but those two aspects of my cultural identity are inextricably intertwined in me as a whole, single being. I view the world, live life, and communicate with others as a Chinese American, not today as Chinese and tomorrow as American. Although in one context I may behave more as a Chinese than an American and in another I may be more American, neither of my cultural aspects is ever completely absent. And, even when an aspect is not readily visible in my behavior, it is always there, informing my decisions, my actions, and my understandings of events and situations. This duality makes me flexible, adaptable, and open-minded in viewing the world, communicating with people, and dealing with different situations in life or at work. And I still rarely dream only in English or Chinese.

My coauthors and I translanguage all the time in our everyday lives: when talking with our families at home; when communicating with relatives and friends across states, countries, and continents; when engaging with the various communities in which we belong; and even when doing our academic work. So, for example, Xenia uses a mix of Cypriot Greek, Greek, and English when talking to her 8-year-old son, Erik, but uses English when English-only speakers are around, so they can be included in the interaction. However, she purposefully uses Greek when she wants to caution or reprimand Erik in English-speaking contexts to protect him from the embarrassment of being scolded in public. Similarly, Xenia's interactions with Cyprus-based colleagues involve intense translanguaging, utilizing features from all three of their common languages, only switching to a single language when composing for a specific publication.

Xiaodi lived the first seven years of his life in China, speaking Mandarin Chinese with his friends and family. Immediately following his 7th birthday, he came to the United States and entered a new language environment. English soon became his most proficient language, the sanctioned privileged vernacular in his new world. In middle school, he studied Latin, and in high school he learned Spanish. In his mind, sometimes he crosses between the three languages of English, Chinese, and Spanish. He lives now with his bilingual wife, with whom he speaks Chinese laced with English, as well as his in-laws, who are monolingual Mandarin Chinese speakers. When he converses with neighbors or English-speaking friends and colleagues, he crosses over to English. Translanguaging has always been an intricate part of his linguistic life. For all of us, the notion of translanguaging has deepened our understanding not only of ourselves as bilinguals or trilinguals, but also of the emergent bilingual students we work with.

CHALLENGES IN SCHOOL FOR EMERGENT BILINGUALS

Thanks to our experience in schools with teachers and students, we are well aware of the situations of emergent bilinguals in our schools, and have witnessed the challenges they encounter in their learning. In pull-out ESL programs we saw students working hard to learn English language skills but, when they returned to their mainstream classrooms, they were lost regarding what was going on around them, and always trailed behind their peers academically. Year after year, they remained labeled as English learners, and many just bided their time until they could drop out of school. With the push-in ESL model, we have seen ESL teachers struggle to cover all the students who needed help at different grades in different subjects. Even when the ESL teacher did come into the class to work with a few EBs, she often served more as a remedial tutor, helping EBs with their schoolwork. Some of these teachers complained they felt like para-professionals rather than licensed ESL teachers, and they could sense that the EBs they worked with felt embarrassed when they had to be pulled aside to be tutored. Both students and teachers felt that the ESL designation carried a stigma, an unwelcomed set of assumptions that branded them as second-class citizens of their school communities.

The teachers and students in transitional bilingual programs we worked with also felt that they shared this stigma. Even though their programs were supposed to help students develop their subject-content knowledge while developing their English proficiency, many teachers and students felt the program was more geared for either beginning or long-term ELs. As a result, instead of affirming their relationship with their home language, many students in these transitional bilingual programs developed resentment or resistance to learning through their home language, along with a sense of shame over their language background. Some parents felt that the bilingual programs isolated their children linguistically, socially, and academically at school, and delayed their children's English development. In a city like New York, where more than 250 different home languages are spoken among students, finding well-trained bilingual teachers is a constant challenge for schools packed with EBs of widely diverse language backgrounds. With the heavy influx of immigrant students into our schools in the past 2 decades, this challenge is now more pronounced than ever nationwide.

In our experience, language separation is often a major cause for the challenges emergent bilinguals encounter in their learning. In most ESL programs, "English-only" is adopted in teaching and learning. Therefore, beginning EBs are kept at the basic-language-skill learning level before they are exposed to any books, learn grade-level content, or write for self-expression and presentation of learning. Research indicates it takes 2–3 years to develop communicative language, and 5–7 or even 10 years to develop academic language (Thomas & Collier, 2002). At this pace, how can EBs ever study with their English-proficient peers or at their appropriate grade level? In this academic journey, the train has moved on, and these EBs are left behind at the station.

A transitional bilingual program is supposed to build emergent bilinguals' content knowledge with their home language at their grade level while developing English proficiency. However, in such home-language-only programs, students not only feel isolated from their English-proficient peers, but also see little connection between what they are learning in the home language classes and the other classes they are in. Therefore, the bilingual program often functions as a school within a school, which has little to do with the rest of the school, and makes the students in the program feel inferior to their peers. Many students either try to get out of transitional bilingual programs or give up, waiting until they are not legally required to be in school anymore.

To confront these challenges encountered by our emergent bilingual students, we argue in this book that the translanguaging model can offer promising solutions. Translanguaging approaches create spaces and opportunities and provide structure for emergent bilinguals to use any languages they choose to maximize their learning and potential. In a translanguaging classroom, students can choose to read texts in a language they can understand; they can discuss their learning with others in one or more languages so they can express their meanings and be understood; and they can draft their writing in their home language and translate their work for all their peers and teacher to comprehend. In this way, students with limited proficiencies in English can effectively use tools from their home languages and home literacies to access grade-level curriculum along with their more-English-proficient peers. Through translanguaging, teachers guide students to develop the school's target language while allowing them to move back and forth between languages in order to deepen their learning and expression.

Effective implementations of translanguaging are strategic and intentional, not simply incidental. In other words, teachers do not just allow translanguaging to "happen" in their classrooms; they plan for it and create instructional spaces in which all students engage in learning new content knowledge at grade level through purposeful translanguaging practices. Within this space, teachers coach and support students to do the following:

- Compare grammar conventions across languages and find vocabulary connections
- Consider which language(s) to use in different situations
- Deliberate on when and how to compose bilingual texts
- Ruminate on the complexities of translation

Ultimately, in a translanguaging classroom all students, including EBs, spend time considering their languages and the language tools at their disposal, and they work toward expanding and honing their skills in all their languages, gaining a metaperspective of human languages. As García and Li (2014) suggest, the translanguaging model can be used in any instructional setting where there are emergent bilinguals: ESL, transitional bilingual, dual language bilingual, or mainstream classrooms. It has the capacity to transform practice to meet challenges, improve literacy and language education for emerging bilinguals, and also prepare all students for the 21st-century globalized, plurilingual world.

OVERVIEW OF THIS BOOK

Drawing on our years of work with emergent bilinguals and our own backgrounds as bilinguals, we explore the teaching and learning experiences of emergent bilinguals in our schools, narrating vivid vignettes from inside and outside classrooms to showcase their living and learning experiences in their communities and in our schools linguistically, academically, and socially. (We have also created a companion website that readers can visit at: http://www.translanguagingforebs.com/) For over 2 decades, we collected countless classroom vignettes and portraits of emergent bilinguals and their teachers in different contexts, classrooms, and circumstances across the United States. We recorded their words, and took note of teaching practices, student performances, and experiences in and out of the classroom. In writing, we knitted and wove these pieces into cohesive narratives that address the aspects and ideas we needed to present regarding the academic and social lives of emergent bilingual students in this country. The experiences depicted in the stories we share constitute a combined reality for emergent bilinguals across the United States. All the names for students and adults used in the book are pseudonyms.

Following this introduction, there are five chapters in this book. Chapter 1 identifies and analyzes persisting issues and challenges in the education of emergent bilinguals, including demographic shifts and policy mandates. In this chapter, we expand our case for translanguaging pedagogy as a promising approach in dealing with these challenges and preparing students for active citizenship in the 21st century. Vignettes showcase everyday language practices of bi/multilinguals and demonstrate the potential of translanguaging in formal teaching and learning contexts.

Chapter 2 addresses academic challenges EBs encounter in their education. Classroom vignettes of EBs in different ESL programs (pull-out, push-in, self-contained) and bilingual programs (transitional and dual language) present and analyze academic challenges EBs face as they attempt to meet grade-level expectations in terms of curriculum and standards. Contrasting vignettes from translanguaging classrooms show how teachers can create space and structures for EBs to maximize their learning potential and to be able to learn complex content at their grade level and develop academic English as needed in learning.

Chapter 3 turns to the social challenges that EBs encounter in school settings. We use stories of EB students to illustrate and analyze the social isolation and stigma they often face in classrooms and school communities due to language hierarchy and separation, as well as the remedial teaching approach in ESL and transitional bilingual programs. Then translanguaging classroom vignettes contrast with the above situations and show how EBs are involved with class activities in different learning settings (ESL or bilingual and mainstream) along with peers with different language backgrounds and English proficiencies.

Chapter 4 addresses challenges teachers and schools face in providing adequate and effective education for EBs from vastly different language and cultural backgrounds. Classroom vignettes of emerging bilingual students demonstrate how, in some settings, these students cannot receive the same support and assistance as other bi/multilingual students due to the lack of resources and personnel in the schools. Later, vignettes of translanguaging classrooms illustrate, in contrast, how teachers structure their teaching with a translanguaging approach to allow students to flexibly use their language strengths to learn from and with each other in these classrooms.

Chapter 5 provides takeaway strategies and practical recommendations for preservice and inservice teachers to implement a translanguaging approach in different educational contexts. In closing, we further demonstrate how translanguaging serves as a promising model in preparing students for 21st-century citizenship.

As a whole, this book introduces translanguaging as a conceptual and instructional model to readers through emergent bilingual students' classroom and real-life experiences and through the voices of students, parents, teachers, and school administrators. It also illustrates how, by activating our students' entire linguistic repertoires as learning tools and resources in our teaching, this instructional model engages emergent bilinguals in rigorous learning in different academic settings, empowers them as learners and language users, and prepares all students for the 21st-century pluralistic world.

CHAPTER 1

Translanguaging
A Promising Approach for the Education of Emergent Bilinguals

Lakshmi is the head of the physician training department of the U.S. branch of a multinational medical device company. She is getting ready for her monthly teleconference with her peers who are responsible for other geographic areas her company serves. Though she has been in this position for several years, she is still in awe of the fact that she has such a close collaborative relationship with colleagues who live and work in different parts of the world. The first to join the teleconference is Arjun, her colleague from India. They greet each other in Hindi and then they continue chatting in a mixture of Hindi and English about some new developments in a joint project. Though Lakshmi grew up in the United States and Arjun in India, they are both proficient in Hindi and in English, as well as in one nonstandard Hindi dialect each.

Soon, they are joined by colleagues from Germany, the UK, South Africa, and Hong Kong, and they all begin to work through their agenda. The conversation is in English, though it is clear from accents, word choices, and other particularities that, in this interaction, the participants are using a variety of Englishes. Beyond English, however, other languages are also visibly featured in the interaction in several ways:

- Several of the slides and diagrams that participants share in presenting their work and ideas are bilingual.
- The notes individual participants take during the interaction are often a mixture of English and other languages.
- Jointly crafted artifacts such as training modules and public relations materials that are to be translated for use across their different settings are vetted for appropriateness, relevance, and clarity, both in the local varieties of English as well as other local languages.

In the example above, a group of professionals leverages their knowledge across different languages to communicate meaningfully and effectively in a globalized, interconnected community. Their interactions are facilitated by digital, 21st-century technologies, allowing these individuals with diverse cultural backgrounds and linguistic resources to think and talk together, as well as create and share a variety of texts. Their communication is, of course, made possible by the fact that they all have enough of a common language to be able to understand what their peers are saying and to contribute to the interaction productively. It is important to note, however, that there does not seem to be a need to establish and regulate the use of one "correct" variety of English for collaboration to thrive; what is important is that they can understand one another and accomplish the goals of their meeting. It is also notable that all participants speak other languages beyond English and that this knowledge is actively harnessed as a resource to develop and refine their joint projects, as well as in shaping and enhancing their interpersonal relationships and networking. Through this vignette, translanguaging emerges as a powerful practice for effective participation in 21st-century contexts.

A key question, however, arises: Does current practice in our educational system(s) prepare young people for participation in this world? In this chapter, we argue that the commonly used monolingual approaches to education with their focus on the acquisition of a regional standard dialect and their single-minded pursuit of literacy in that language are inadequate. We propose instead that a translanguaging orientation to teaching and learning provides a promising 21st-century education framework for children whose heritage, or home, languages are different from the language of instruction at school, as well as for the education of all learners. To contextualize this discussion, we begin by reviewing demographic shifts in immigration to the United States and the resulting presence of emergent bilinguals in U.S. schools. We make the case that the current U.S. educational system is fundamentally monolingual in its orientation, and summarize persisting challenges to the education of EBs in the current system. We then describe how globalization and advances in technology and communication demand the development of different kinds of literacy skills that cannot be adequately developed through monolingual models of education. To support our case for translanguaging pedagogy, we present examples from the everyday language practices of bi/multilinguals and link them to formal teaching and learning contexts, with a particular focus on 21st-century literacy demands.

DEMOGRAPHIC SHIFTS IN U.S. IMMIGRATION

The United States is often described as a nation of immigrants. This is a country that people from all over the world perceive as a land of opportunity —a place where ambitious individuals who are willing to work hard could "make it" regardless of their social and economic pedigrees. Despite these generalized perceptions, however, immigration to the United States has never been an even stream of newcomers from all over the world. Rather, social, political, and economic circumstances and crises in countries of origin (e.g., wars, persecution, extreme poverty), in combination with quotas and restrictive immigration policies in the United States, led to the development of distinct immigration waves. Each inbound group of immigrants has experienced different educational approaches as emergent bilinguals (Wasem, 2013).

First Wave

During the revolutionary and post-revolutionary periods of the country (1790–1820), immigration was dominated by British settlers, but also included German, Dutch, and French nationals. Although English was the unofficial national language during that time, early bilingual curricula were created to serve the German, Dutch, and French communities (Rong & Preissle, 2015).

Second Wave

The second wave of immigration lasted from 1849 to 1860, and immigrants during this time were predominantly from Germany, Ireland, Scandinavia, and Eastern Europe. Notable educators during this era like Horace Mann and Henry Barnard advocated for universal public schooling with the explicit task of turning these immigrants into "Americans" (Bandiera, Mohnen, Rasul, & Viarengo, 2001). Immigrants were aggressively socialized and taught only English at public schools. During this time, biculturalism was seen as unpatriotic and un-American, and teachers even propagated Social Darwinism in extolling the "American ethnicity" (Rory, 2012).

Third Wave

The third wave of immigration spans the years between the Civil War and the beginning of the First World War (1860–1919). During this period, immigration burgeoned, mainly from Southern and Eastern Europe. Chinese and Japanese people also arrived on the West Coast to meet the labor needs in the agricultural and railroad industries. The new immigrants and their places of origin were often viewed with suspicion and distrust, and were perceived as potentially dangerous to "the good order" of the country (Public Broadcasting System, 2001). In response, the United States adopted a series of wholesale measures like the Chinese Exclusion Act of 1882, which prohibited all immigration of Chinese laborers, and the Immigration Act of 1924, which applied national origin quotas to immigrants and effectively excluded immigrants from Asia (de Jong, 2011).

Another response to this new diversity was cementing an assimilationist, English-centered Americanization movement. In fact, by 1906, the United

States was requiring English fluency as part of its test for naturalized citizenship. Meanwhile, urban public schools were becoming socialization and homogenization hubs, with centralized curricula solely in English. The immigrant children in these schools became the first recognized English learners. However, the only accommodation they received was getting placed in lower grade levels than their peers. Other than that, they participated in regular, full English-submersion classrooms without any special instructional support. This "sink or swim" strategy, as de Jong (2011) and Pavlenko (2002) report, proved wholly ineffective in providing sufficient language or content instruction, and many immigrant children either failed to graduate high school or graduated with limited literacy skills. However, the booming economy allowed for the gainful employment of even low-skilled laborers, thus helping proliferate the myth that English submersion and severance from heritage cultures, including home languages, is a key component of socioeconomic mobility and, ultimately, of making it in America (de Jong, 2011).

Fourth Wave

The fourth wave began in earnest by 1965 and extends into the present era (Fix & Passel, 2003; Rong & Preissle, 2015). The newest tide of immigrants largely hails from Asia and Latin America. There has also been a spike in Arab immigration from the Middle East and North Africa, with migrants seeking refuge from war and political turmoil. These newcomers bring distinct non-European languages and customs that provide new challenges for the nation's educational and linguistic policies. There have been approximately 14 million new immigrants to the United States in the 1st decade of the 21st century, making it the most newcomers in a decade ever (Camarota, 2011).

A notable difference between past immigration waves and the current one is the destinations of the immigrants. Although in the past new immigrants had settled in coastal or midwestern urban centers and congregated in ethnic communities, the new destinations are areas of the South. The states with the highest rates of immigrant population growth are Alabama (92%), South Carolina (88%), Tennessee (82%), Arkansas (79%), Kentucky (75%), North Carolina (67%), and Georgia (63%). Nonetheless, California, New York, Texas, and Florida remain the top destinations in the raw numbers of new immigrants (Camarota, 2011).

Recent immigrants make up a sizeable segment of the emergent bilinguals in U.S. schools today and their educational needs are of crucial significance to the educational systems that serve them. However, it is also important to remember that recent immigrants are not the only kind of emergent bilingual learner who needs language support. Indeed, according to Capps et al. (2005), more than half of all EBs attending U.S. schools were actually born in the United States and, among them, considerable percentages are third-generation Americans. The experience of being a U.S.-born EB has its own particularities and creates distinct academic and socio-emotional needs (see Chapter 3).

A FUNDAMENTALLY MONOLINGUAL EDUCATIONAL SYSTEM

When considering the education of emergent bilinguals, teachers typically ask questions like:

- How can we teach students who speak diverse languages in our classrooms?
- How can we scaffold their learning so they can make academic progress despite their limited proficiency in English?
- How can we help them study along with their proficient English-speaking peers with the same grade curricula so they can participate in classroom activities and feel part of our learning community?

And indeed, much of what educators do in schools in response to the unique needs of EBs seeks to address these very questions.

As discussed above, the education of emergent bilinguals has for decades focused on enabling them to become more like native speakers of English; in other words, on assimilating them into the presumed "melting pot" of American society. These days, American education can boast significant strides since the early days of the Americanization movement: Multicultural pedagogy is widely accepted as valuable, and sophisticated support services for emergent bilinguals are designed and implemented. Nonetheless, the unwavering objective of much of schooling for EBs remains their linguistic assimilation into American English. From this perspective, the languages and the cultural tools EBs possess have no relevance or value in schools, and they do not appear to be worth developing any further. All the students need is to develop their competence in English and to use that language alone in building their academic knowledge and skills. This perspective reveals a monolingual orientation to language and literacy education as it unquestioningly casts English as the sole language in which school learning can be pursued.

A monolingual orientation to language/literacy education is quite a pervasive ideology in the United States, as well as in second language acquisition (SLA), foreign language, and bilingual education fields worldwide. As such, it influences public opinion, policy decisions, and, of course, educational curricula and practice. Monolingual orientations assume that each language a speaker knows has its own distinct and autonomous linguistic repertoire, its own separate area in the speaker's brain. As the speaker has increasing experiences with a certain language, its distinct linguistic repertoire grows, bringing about proficiency. Since each language is presumed to have its own separate repertoire, any language knowledge beyond the target language (i.e., English in the United States) is irrelevant. Consequently, the target language becomes the focus of instruction, and all teachers' efforts center on students becoming competent and confident users of English. Under some circumstances, as in transitional bilingual programs, other languages are allowed to enter the classroom but only as temporary scaffolds. As students' proficiency in English grows, the need to bring in other languages declines and eventually disappears altogether. Other than that, a school really does not have space for students' home languages and their home communities' ways of telling stories, sharing histories, composing poetry, or building an argument.

ESL programs with either pull-out or push-in models, sheltered instruction, transitional bilingual programs, and newcomer schools steadfastly focus on enabling students to study their grade-level curriculum while acquiring English. In many ways, a key measure of success for emergent bilinguals in these settings is how fast they can relinquish the need to receive special services. And indeed, evidence suggests that each of these approaches does benefit EBs in this journey. However, there is also ample research pointing to persistent challenges that hamper success.

PERSISTENT EDUCATIONAL CHALLENGES FOR EMERGENT BILINGUALS

Emergent bilinguals (identified in schools as "English learners") are a fast-increasing population in American schools. According to the Institute of Education Sciences (IES), in 2014–2015 there were 4.8 million EL students in K–12 U.S. schools, representing 9.5% of the total student population and 300,000 more ELs than in 2004–2005 (National Center for Education Statistics [NCES], 2017). In 2007, more than one in five children spoke a language other than English at home, and of these, about a quarter had difficulties speaking English (Ryan, 2013).

Examinations of the academic trajectories of English learners in U.S. schools suggest that there are currently many issues with their education (Menken, Hudson, & Leung, 2014; Plough & Garcia, 2015; Sullivan, 2011). Some of these issues include the following:

- ELs often struggle academically and tend to underperform their English-proficient peers in national and state exams (Snyder & Dillow, 2013).
- ELs are disproportionately identified as having learning disabilities (Sanatullova-Allison & Robison-Young, 2016; Sullivan, 2011).

- ELs have worryingly high dropout rates (Sheng, Sheng, & Anderson, 2011).

Emergent bilinguals often struggle because they are pressed to learn and immediately use the new language to acquire content knowledge and meet grade-level expectations. Educational backgrounds, age of arrival, home/community environment, school resources/programs, district/state policy, and teacher quality all impact their learning. In what follows, we will briefly discuss persistent challenges EBs encounter in their education, including limited access to suitable educational resources, limited access to teachers prepared to work with them, and inadequate assessments of their knowledge (see Chapter 4 for a discussion of challenges faced by schools serving EBs).

Limited Access to Appropriate Resources and a Supportive Learning Environment

In many school districts across the country, there may not be adequate support for EBs, especially those whose formal education was interrupted. The situation varies from classroom to classroom, school to school, district to district, and state to state. In some school districts, due to lack of resources, a single ESL teacher has to travel across schools in the district to serve between 100 and 200 EBs who speak different home languages and who have varying education backgrounds and language abilities. Without adequate support, EBs often find themselves in learning environments that are not adequately set up to meet their needs. Many schools may lack sufficient reading materials at different levels, genres, and topics in home languages and in English. This can be particularly problematic for older EBs who may find themselves stuck reading books that match their reading proficiency in English but have content well below their age and intellectual levels.

Another persistent challenge is the lack of opportunities to work and socialize with mainstream peers in substantial ways. Research shows that many EBs are confined to their own ethnic communities and attend schools where 30% or more of the student population are also EBs (Fix & Passel, 2003). This isolation becomes even more accentuated through the common practices of pulling EBs out for instruction or having them work separately on modified activities in the mainstream classroom. As we will discuss in Chapter 3, whether at home or at school, EBs in monolingually oriented settings often have limited opportunities to socialize or study with English speakers and to practice either their social or academic language.

Shortage of Teachers with ESL Training

In many states, EBs are fully included or spend the majority of the day in regular classrooms, studying the same curriculum as their English-proficient peers. With increasing total numbers of EBs, along with their growing presence in schools that did not have EBs in the past, more and more general education teachers are called upon to meet the diverse linguistic and pedagogical demands of learners who are not proficient in English (Calderón, Slavin, & Sánchez, 2011). Although some traditional "gateway" states such as New York and Arizona have ESL requirements for teacher certification, most states do not (Education Commission of the States, 2014). As a result, many EBs are placed with classroom teachers who do not have sufficient training to effectively facilitate their learning. When questioned about their preparation, mainstream teachers report feeling "ill-prepared" to meet the needs of the linguistically diverse students in their classrooms (Calderón et al., 2011). To teach EBs, teachers need to understand their complexity as learners, the theory and practice related to second language learning and bilingual education, and instructional strategies to scaffold EBs in learning content knowledge while developing new language skills.

Inadequate Assessment of Educational Status

Although EBs represent an extremely diverse student population in terms of their education and home language backgrounds, in most school districts they are placed at a grade level based on their chronological age. Because of their limited proficiency in English and, for some, the lack of adequate formal education, they struggle to learn or feel too overwhelmed to make appropriate progress to meet grade-level requirements. Often these students are overdiagnosed as learning disabled (Sullivan, 2011). Conversely, many EBs who do have learning disabilities are not appropriately diagnosed and end up not receiving the support they need for their learning.

An additional complication is that the lackluster achievement of EBs on tests seems to be primarily contingent on English language needs rather than their command of the content being tested (Abedi, 2008). Based on accountability expectations across the United States, EBs are often expected to take and pass the same standardized tests that their mainstream peers are required to take, which are created with English-proficient students in mind. Though it is now common practice for students who are identified as English learners to receive testing accommodations, several scholars report that success on these tests still presupposes high proficiency in English and that these accommodations do not provide adequate support (Hutchinson & Hadjioannou, 2017; Martiniello, 2008; Schissel, 2014).

Another challenge EBs encounter relates to the English language proficiency (ELP) tests they take to be placed in ESL services (also known as English language development [ELD] services), determine their progress in learning English, and eventually exit them out of ESL programs. These ELP tests are designed to assess EBs' knowledge of English and place them at different levels of English proficiency. So, for example, WIDA's *ACCESS for ELLs 2.0* ELP test, which is used widely in the United States, places students in one of six levels of English proficiency. Though this test does also break down EBs' performance in the language domains of listening, speaking, reading, and writing, it still fails to capture significant aspects of EBs' profiles as learners (WIDA Consortium, 2018). Consider, for instance, two 10-year-old students whose test results place them on WIDA's Emerging Level (2) of English proficiency:

- One is the child of two professionals who recently began their doctoral studies in a U.S. university, and was an exemplary student at her previous school.
- The other, born in the United States, is the child of elementary-educated migrant workers who have to move to a different state every few months. As a result, he often misses school for months at a time.

Arguably, the instructional needs of these two students are quite different; however, the single dimension of English language proficiency of the Level 2 label fails to capture the true complexity of their circumstances.

Implications of These Issues

The issues faced by EBs in American schools are inextricably related to the bureaucracies that are supposed to help facilitate their educational attainment. Over the years, a large and intricate system of standards, tests, instructional and reporting mandates, and service models has been put in place to manage the educational experience of students identified as ELs. With the exception of dual language bilingual models, which work toward sustained bilingualism and biliteracy, most service models strive to rapidly move EBs to a level of English language proficiency that would allow them to participate in regular education settings without any specialized support. These days, educators often talk about not only accepting but also celebrating diversity and about making diverse experiences and points of view a cornerstone of the education system. However, the policies and educational practice that shape EBs' classroom experiences have a decisively assimilationist essence.

Indeed, in the current context of the Common Core State Standards (CCSS) and standardized testing, EB students' ability to successfully navigate these expectations has become a vital issue (Kibler, Walqui, & Bunch, 2015), as they are increasingly expected to take and pass high-stakes tests in English as early as a year after their arrival in the United States. The demands of the Common Core are more strenuous than previous standards and require deeper comprehension of texts, more scaffolding of learning, and the use of texts of increasing complexity. These requisites put more pressure on EBs' capabilities and prove more taxing for their long-term success. For example, in California and New York, two states with the highest proportions of students identified as ELs, only 25% and 29%, respectively, met grade-level expectations in the 4th grade, and less than 25% of middle school EL graduates performed at or above the 8th-grade level. Emergent bilingual students scored markedly worse on the California Standardized Test, especially in language arts where, in the 2nd grade, there was a 20% disparity between EBs and their English-proficient counterparts (45% EB passing rate versus 65% English-proficient passing rate). Even more concerning, however, was that by the 11th grade, only 6% of EBs meet the standards, while 54% of English-proficient speakers were deemed sufficiently proficient (Plough & Garcia, 2015).

Unfortunately, New York and California are not alone in these worrisome results. Across the United States, EBs perform markedly worse on a number of educational assessments, which creates a notable achievement gap between them and their English-proficient peers. Poor academic performance often translates to decreased desire and opportunities for postsecondary education and may lead to lower-paying jobs. Even before high school graduation, however, frustrating experiences with schooling and poor performance on standardized exams lead many EBs to lose hope and interest in completing their K–12 education. According to data from NCES (2015) for the 2013–2014 school year, the graduation rate of EBs was only 62.6%, the lowest of all subgroups considered. In contrast, the overall graduation rate was 82.3%. And, while the dropout rates for English-proficient students fluctuate year to year and from state to state, the numbers for EBs consistently run about 10 percentage points higher. Apart from academic frustration, dropping out of school may also be related to a host of nonacademic factors for EB students. For example, these youths often need to find full-time employment to meet the financial needs of their families, whereas others need to care for younger siblings and/or assume other household responsibilities.

Since the 19th century, the United States has been operating under the assumption that the best route both for individuals and society is monolingualism, and the educational system has been structured accordingly. One of the core objectives of educational policy and practice regarding EBs has been helping them develop their proficiency in English so they can be academically successful in English-only settings. Therefore, EBs' other languages are often excluded from school learning, and even when they are invited in, they are typically used as a temporary crutch for content or English language learning. However, are these longstanding assumptions indeed the best way to guide the education of this student population? The persistent challenges we identified above suggest a need to rethink current practices and question the underlying monolingual assumptions and guiding principles of the current models for educating emergent bilinguals.

BEING LITERATE IN A GLOBALIZED AND DIGITALIZED WORLD

Beyond the persisting challenges with the education of EBs, another important consideration that should inform the critical review of our educational system's monolingual orientation is the evolving expectations of what it
means to be literate in a globalized and digitalized world. A few decades
ago, computers were scarce and took up entire rooms; oral communication
across distances was possible, but costly; and there was no such thing as
simultaneous written communication. People and economies, as well as professional and social networks, were geographically bound. These days, we
carry the power of the Internet in our pockets and videoconferencing is free-
ly available to anyone with a webcam and an Internet connection. Emails,
text messages, and tweets are delivered around the globe with a click of the
send button and social media have the capacity to introduce us and keep us
closely connected to wide networks of people.

In a time when individuals can readily talk and collaborate with people
across the globe; when reading and writing involves engagement not only
with written language but also with images, sounds, and video; when em-
ployees can telecommute to work; and when team members can collaborate
on a project across countries and borders, the understanding of literacy,
language proficiency, and what it means to be a highly functional literate
person is surely not the same as it was 30 years ago. Being able to effectively
communicate with such varied audiences and through such complex texts
necessitates a skill set that seems to go well beyond being a really good
user of a single regional standard and of a local literate culture. Rather, as
illustrated in the vignette that opened this chapter, the evolving circumstances of communication seem to demand a more agile, flexible approach that
involves familiarity with different ways of communicating and the ability
to shape what is said in response to the expectations of each situation. In
the 21st-century globalized world, all citizens should be prepared to operate within a plurilingual setting and with cosmopolitan mindsets (Zaidi

& Rowsell, 2017). This could mean becoming literate in more than one language, being able to communicate with people with different language backgrounds, and being able to appreciate culturally different ways of communication and expression and to work with people with different perspectives and worldviews. Monolingual approaches to language and to education are clearly not equipped to prepare learners in this way. Translanguaging, on the other hand, seems to be well poised to respond to this challenge, as it acknowledges all the language resources of individuals and purposefully seeks to develop and expand all aspects of their linguistic repertoire.

BILINGUAL PRACTICE AND THE PROMISE OF TRANSLANGUAGING

Imagine language repertoires as rooms in a house. With a monolingual perspective, every language you know has its own separate room in the house, with its own furniture, decorations, and gadgets. Switching from language to language would be like moving from one room to another. Once you are in a room, you only have access to the items there. You can always cross the threshold to switch to another language in a different room, but once in a room, you are pretty much confined to using what is there.

In contrast, when language knowledge is viewed through a translanguaging perspective, the analogy changes drastically. Instead of imagining different rooms for each language, there is a single, multifunctional room for all your linguistic knowledge. There you have access to all language features and tools in your repertoire and can flexibly select and use what you need at any given moment. You may not use every single thing in the room simultaneously, but it is all there within reach.

When emergent bilinguals are taught using a monolingual approach, the focus is exclusively on the development of the target language or language of instruction. This practice assumes that becoming proficient in English is a fundamental prerequisite to EBs' future success and that their home languages are far less important or even completely irrelevant to their formal schooling. Continuing the room analogy, through a monolingual approach, the only focus is on furnishing and equipping the one room that matters. As we discussed in the Introduction, some may even believe that if EBs cut themselves off from their home languages, their language and academic learning would have a better chance to flourish. However, evidence suggests that individuals have a single, unified language repertoire that encompasses the linguistic features of all their languages and they naturally translanguage to fit their needs for communication in different contexts and with different people. This means that, even when bilingual individuals choose to speak in a single language, they bring to the table all their languages—all their language tools are in the same room. As García, Johnson, and Seltzer (2017) note, "When bilingual students write or create something new, they may filter certain features of their linguistic repertoires to create the *product*, but the *process* will always be bilingual" (p. 17). We illustrate this concept in the following section.

Translanguaging in the Daily Lives of Bilinguals

Sociocognitive theories of learning and educational research have often studied children as they are learning in natural settings to draw conclusions about how to best facilitate their learning when they are in classrooms. In the same vein, Ofelia García (2009) suggests that to better understand how to teach emergent bilinguals, it would be instructive to examine how bilinguals use language in their daily, authentic interactions. In the vignette below, we observe a conversation between Xenia and her 8-year-old son Erik, both of whom speak Greek and English, to see how they are using the languages they know to communicate and relate to each other:

> Erik is a big fan of Norse mythology. He and his mom have read several books together involving the Norse gods. Xenia is herself a mythology buff, who as a child had spent countless hours reading about the myths of the Greco-Roman pantheon and those of their Norse counterparts. While they are reading a chapter from one of Riordan's (2015) Magnus Chase books, Erik comments, "If I was one of those gods, I think I'd want to be Frey or Thor. Thor is strong and he has a hammer and Frey is the god of summer and he has a sword that fights by itself. Which one of the goddesses do you want to be?" "Καμιά, νομίζω [I don't think I want to be any one of them]," Xenia responds. "The Norse made their male gods strong and gave them cool adventures, but their goddesses are not really that interesting." "Oh, come on," Erik counters. "Μπορείς να είσαι η Frigg ή η Freya [You can be Frigg or Freya]." "Μπα [Nah]," insists Xenia, "Προτιμώ να είμαι η Αθηνά [I'd rather be Athena]."

In the example above, both speakers are bilingual in Greek and in English. To an outside observer, it seems that their conversation primarily involves English, though Greek pops up in some of the utterances. In the past, when looking at the behavior of bilingual speakers, we have used exactly this outside perspective to describe what they are doing as *code-switching, code-mixing,* or *code-meshing.* Though there are some differences in the meanings of these terms, they all look at the behavior of bilinguals through the lens of formal language codes that are defined and separate. So, for instance, when looking at the conversation above through this outside perspective, it looks like the speakers are moving across two distinct languages; the conversation begins utilizing language features identified as English, and then the speakers start using features that are compatible with the code called the Greek language.

However, when looking at this episode from the perspective of the bilingual speakers themselves, the view is quite different. What appear to be two different, named languages to the outside world are, to the bilingual speakers, simply the language features appropriate and relevant to this conversation. As García and her colleagues (2017) would say, both speakers are using the "entwined linguistic features" of their single language repertoire to make meaning, though "countries, schools, dictionaries, and grammar books classify [them] as different languages" (p. 18). The speakers know that because of their shared language backgrounds, when they talk to each other, they can use a wide range of shared linguistic features to express their thoughts and be understood. Since they've been reading a text written in English, it makes sense for them to respond to it using language features that relate to the text. Similarly, Greek features are also appropriate in this conversation as it is their shared language of family intimacy and Xenia is very purposefully trying to infuse it in Erik's environment. Instead of getting hung up on formal borders between codes of language, they focus on the overall communicative practice of language. In other words, they are *translanguaging*.

Interestingly, later in the day when Erik told the story of this conversation to his father, he made sure to select language features consistent with English, since that is the only language his father speaks. Notably, Erik concluded his story with, "and then she said that she'd rather be Αθηνά [Athena], but I don't know who that is." In this retelling, the only Greek feature that remained in Erik's story was the name Αθηνά (Athena), which Xenia had said in Greek and Erik did not know its equivalent in English. As a bilingual speaker, Erik knows that, to communicate effectively, he needs to select and use language features that match the needs of each situation. Being understood by his dad is significant, so he uses his translanguaging skills to translate the Greek parts of the conversation into English, even putting a disclaimer on the one word he could not translate. This is consistent with many studies that "have shown that the language use of bilinguals responds to their communicative and affective intent, as well as to the situation and the interlocutor" (García, 2009, p. 47).

In discussing this vignette so far, we have focused on what the two speakers actually said. However, in order for a conversation to take place, speakers do a lot of meaning-making work that is not readily visible to an observer; they work to make sense of what others are saying by connecting it to their background knowledge and experiences, and then they use their knowledge and experiences to figure out what to say in response. To dig a bit deeper into that idea, let's look beyond the words spoken and zoom in to what Xenia and Erik did in this short conversation. They used their ability to comprehend the story they were reading, made intertextual connections with other texts they had read in the past, analyzed what they knew of the Norse gods, and contrasted it to their personal preferences to conclude which god or goddess each felt more affinity to. All these meaning-making activities are important literacy skills that are processed using language tools. Even if Erik and Xenia had used only Greek or only English in their conversation, since they are bilingual, the literacy skills they enacted to comprehend, analyze, compare, and synthesize were supported by the entwined language features of all their languages, not simply the language features specific to the language used to express their ideas. Since they are bilinguals with a single language repertoire, their process is bilingual as well.

At the end of the day, when supporting the literacy learning of all students, teachers want to help them achieve a host of language performance objectives. García et al. (2017) acknowledge that several of those objectives can be *language specific*—that is, objectives that refer to "speakers' exclusive use of features from a named language (e.g., Spanish, Mandarin, English) to perform classroom tasks" (p. 80). However, the authors also remind us that many of the literacy skills people use in their lives, and which teachers aspire to help students develop as part of their schooling, involve performance that is not associated with one specific language. These are called *general linguistic performance* skills and they involve "speakers' use of oral and written language to express complex thoughts (e.g., to explain, persuade, argue, compare and contrast, find text evidence, give directions, or recount events) drawing on the full features of their linguistic repertoires" (p. 80).

The notion of general linguistic performance skills, and their inextricable connection to the full spectrum of bilingual speakers' language repertoires, is very significant as it strongly suggests that educators should strive to engage all of students' language tools in the process of learning. At the same time, it reveals that the common practices of marginalizing or completely excluding some of the students' languages from the process of education are misguided and potentially harmful to students' learning opportunities. Take, for example, an English-only 3rd-grade classroom where students are only allowed to use the English they know to do their work, without any space for home languages to participate in the processes of learning. It's science time and the class is working on "describ[ing] the characteristics of living things that help to identify and classify them" (Pennsylvania Learning/SAS Standard 3.1.3.A1). Emergent bilinguals who may be perfectly capable of comparing living and nonliving things, creating criteria for membership in a category, and using those criteria to determine classifications may not have the chance to practice and hone these significant literacy skills because of their limited proficiency in English. Instead, they are likely to find themselves answering yes or no questions about whether different things are living or nonliving, or completing fill-in-the-gap worksheets with core vocabulary.

Compare this to a translanguaging classroom where students are supported in using the full range of their language repertoires. In such a classroom, though the lesson would still have language-specific objectives expecting students to use English in performing certain tasks, it would also include several general linguistic performance objectives that would leverage all their languages. In such a classroom, students would be provided access to reading materials and videos in their home languages and in English, and they would be encouraged to take notes and begin drafting their criteria lists in the language(s) of their choice. They may even have the chance to collaborate with peers in developing bilingual posters showcasing how a butterfly, a rock, or a mouse fits their criteria. Students would still need to learn and use the English academic vocabulary associated with the lesson and they would potentially still be expected to produce a final project written exclusively in English. However, to cycle back to an earlier quote from García et al. (2017), their process is honored as fundamentally bilingual, even if they are expected to filter certain features of their language repertoire to respond to the monolingual expectations of a specific task.

Translanguaging and Social Justice

The way we choose to look shapes how we understand what we are seeing. Monolingual perspectives to education and social life create rigid hierarchies of language, which strongly privilege certain language varieties (American English in the case of the United States) and marginalize other languages and language varieties and the people who speak them. When we educators look at emergent bilinguals through a monolingual perspective, we see them for what they cannot yet do: They are not yet proficient in English and therefore they are bound to have a hard time acquiring the knowledge and skills necessary to meet their grade-level standards. Through this lens, our duty is clear: Teach them English as quickly as possible. Their identity and socioemotional state as bilinguals in the world are not part of the picture.

On the other hand, when we look at emergent bilinguals through a plurilingual translanguaging perspective, our understanding of what we are seeing is quite different. Emergent bilinguals are not simply learners of English; they are bilinguals (or multilinguals) in the making. As a result, our duty is to help them become competent and confident bilinguals, who are empowered to build strong bilingual identities and to work toward shaping a more just and equitable society, where who they are and what they know is understood as valuable and treated with respect.

García et al. (2017) remind us that using language is not simply a matter of putting words together to express our thoughts; it also involves complex social knowledge and understandings. They posit that "when we *language*, we are performing a series of social practices and actions that link us to what we want and who we believe we are" (p. 162). Through translanguaging pedagogy, we expand students' options for how they use their languages to learn and express themselves. However, those choices have social meanings and consequences. Therefore, in a translanguaging classroom, it is also important to create spaces to discuss the power relations in the society around us—power relations that privilege certain language choices and the people who make them, while at the same time marginalizing others. Such discussions can cultivate students' critical consciousness and spur them to not only identify inequity and oppressive social practices, but also envision and enact reparative practices toward social justice.

So, for example, in translanguaging classrooms students can ask and explore questions about common stereotypes regarding different languages and their speakers (particularly against the languages spoken by people of color), as well as the history of those stereotypes. They may also wonder about recent constitutional amendments at the state level that set English as the official state language, and other policy initiatives for limiting the use of languages other than English at the federal and state levels (Hutchinson & Hadjioannou, 2017). They may even look critically at representations of different language communities and of nonmainstream people in the texts they are reading, and work to rewrite those representations with an eye to authenticity, fairness, and equity.

In translanguaging classrooms, with teachers committed to critical literacy and social justice, such conversations are not only allowed to happen, but teachers actively design the physical space, their instruction, and their assessments to purposefully nurture and support students as they are questioning the world around them, and work toward making it better (García et al., 2017).

CONCLUSION

Ultimately, what we are proposing is that translanguaging is not only a promising instructional model for specifically teaching EBs but also a valuable approach for the literacy education of *all* students. This model purposefully and systematically uses students' linguistic strengths to develop their content knowledge, language skills, and critical awareness of their social contexts. It adopts the flexible manner in which bi/multilinguals strategically utilize the language resources that are of most use to them at any given moment, and envisions plurilingualism for the future of all. Translanguaging models can be deployed in any education settings for EBs: English as a new language, transitional bilingual, dual language bilingual, and mainstream. As suggested above and as we will argue through the chapters that follow, translanguaging seems to be an urgently needed new direction in the education of EBs, which has the capacity to alleviate many of the challenges that characterize currently existing models. In addition, translanguaging pedagogy can serve as a valuable direction for mainstream education, helping monolingual students become consciously aware of their linguistic repertoire and giving them opportunities to expand their communicative competence and open their minds to other languages, ways of expression, and perspectives.

This education, with an understanding of children as emerging plurilinguals who are continuously expanding and developing their linguistic repertoire, strategically utilizes all the linguistic and sociocognitive tools at their disposal. All of their languages are understood as part of the same linguistic repertoire "from which they select features strategically to communicate effectively" (García, 2011, p. 1). In this education, students are encouraged and supported in "the harmonious development of [their] plurilingual competence through a coherent, transversal and integrated approach that takes into account all the languages in learners' plurilingual repertoire and their respective functions" (Council of Europe, Language Policy Division, 2006, p. 5). Rejecting assimilationist agendas that demand that all students "blend in" and adopt the mainstream monolingual and monocultural identities, this education brings the cultural capitals of the students to the forefront of the educational process. Translanguaging understands all languages as equally powerful communication tools and problematizes notions of language hierarchies. All students are invited to contribute their ways of words, cultural knowledge, problem-solving strategies, worldviews, and experiences on their path to becoming confident and knowledgeable global citizens.

CHAPTER 2

Meeting Academic Challenges

There are numerous success stories of emergent bilinguals arriving in U.S. schools as young immigrants who manage to become very successful students, get accepted into prestigious colleges with hefty scholarships, and become prosperous professionals who make their distinctive mark on the various industries and institutions that employ them. However, this is not the typical story of emergent bilinguals who attend U.S. schools. Indeed, as discussed in Chapter 1, careful examinations of how EBs fare in U.S. schools paint a rather disheartening picture. The statistics on academic performance on nationwide and state-level tests are particularly worrisome since they show a persistent gap between the academic performance of students who are designated as English learners and those who are not.

For example, data from the 2013 National Assessment of Educational Progress (NAEP) assessment, a long-running, nationwide assessment of U.S. students, show a large and persistent achievement gap between students identified as ELs and their non-EL peers:

- The proficiency levels of ELs were 23 to 30 percentage points lower than non-ELs in math and in reading.
- Only 3–4% of ELs scored at a proficient level in math and reading.
- 69% of ELs in 8th grade scored below basic in math and 70% below basic in reading.
- 41% of ELs in 4th grade scored below basic in math and 69% below basic in reading.
- The achievement gap between EL and non-EL students has remained pretty consistent over the past 10 years (National Education Association [NEA], 2015).

A similarly bleak picture emerges when considering the performance of EBs on state exams, as we detailed in Chapter 1.

Also worrisome are data suggesting that a significant number of EBs attending U.S. secondary schools become stalled in their progress: They are having a hard time learning English well enough to be considered proficient and are also struggling academically. Known as *long-term ELs*, these students cannot pass the English language proficiency tests even after attending U.S. public schools for 7 years, and have GPAs below 2.0. Though we do not have firm nationwide data on the numbers of long-term ELs, according to Olsen (2014), "estimates are that between one-quarter and one-half of all ELLs who enter U.S. schools in primary grades become Long Term ELLs" (p. 4).

Imagine for a moment being one of the emergent bilinguals whose experience is captured in these statistics. You are in school but you are not learning English at the expected rate, and every day you attend classes but the content taught is consistently out of reach for you. Quizzes, tests, and grades tell you that you are failing. How are you likely to respond? Many EBs in these circumstances end up reshaping their aspirations to match their experience: They give up on school learning as irrelevant or unattainable and, though they hang on long enough to earn their high school diploma, they have little desire or opportunity to go further. Others draw their line even before that, and after losing hope and interest in finishing high school, they drop out.

As educators, we need to ask ourselves some difficult questions:

- Why doesn't our educational system work effectively for EBs, though in past decades so many programs have been specifically established for this student population, such as ESL programs (self-contained, pull-out and push-in models) and bilingual programs (transitional, two-way, or dual language models)?
- What is missing in our instruction?

Education scholars and classroom teachers have been continuing to search for effective ways to serve our emergent bilinguals.

In this chapter, we take a close look at the academic experience of EBs in elementary and middle school classrooms to better understand the forces that create the worrisome statistics reviewed above and consider how *translanguaging* pedagogy can provide a promising alternative. In the next section, we take glimpses into the experiences of emergent bilinguals in school settings that operate using a monolingual perspective—first a pull-out ESL program and then two bilingual programs. Drawing on these experiences, we identify and discuss academic challenges faced by EBs in these settings. The vignettes in monolingual settings are paired with contrasting vignettes showing how these challenges can be effectively addressed in translanguaging classrooms.

CONTRASTING MONOLINGUAL ESL AND TRANSLANGUAGING IN MEETING EMERGENT BILINGUALS' ACADEMIC NEEDS

Rosa, a 4th-Grader in a Pull-Out ESL Program

Rosa leaves her pull-out ESL program and enters her 4th-grade classroom. She sees that the rest of the class is already busy with the science lesson of the day—something about animals and where they live. Every day Rosa leaves her mainstream class for a 45-minute session with her ESL group where they work on English skills such as grammar rules (verb tenses and sentence structures) and vocabulary. As she returns to her regular classroom, Ms. Meyer, her teacher, smiles, hands her a special handout with key-term definitions in both English and Spanish, and motions for her to sit down. Though Rosa has been in the United States for a year and a half and she can speak English with her friends with relative ease, she is having trouble understanding complex stories in English, and following lessons in math and science. Ms. Meyer tries to support her by creating special definition sheets for her, and those do help some, but Rosa finds the speed of everything overwhelming. Though her ESL group is useful in helping with her English, it has little to do with what Ms. Meyer is working on in class, and Rosa feels that she is always walking in in the middle of things. Catching up is hard to do when she is bombarded with a sea of difficult and different English tasks from what she is learning in her ESL room.

Rosa knows a lot about the animals Ms. Meyer is showing on the Smart Board and the class is talking about. Her grandparents own a farm and she helps them care for the animals over the summer. She knows all the animal names in Spanish, but is having a difficult time coming up with their English versions. She wants to tell her class about the time she helped care for her grandparents' cow when she was giving birth, and the excitement of the birth of the calf, and how proud she felt at being a part of that ordeal. But the grammar rules and vocabulary she has been learning in her ESL class do not seem to fit here in her regular class. In her mind, many images are bubbling, but she struggles to put them into words in English. There are so many words she doesn't know, and by the time she figures out one thing, the class has already moved on to something different. She puts her head on her desk and stops listening.

Looking at this vignette from the perspective of the educational system, we can see a number of supports that have been put in place to help Rosa. First, Rosa is pulled out for a period every day into special ESL classes that are meant to accelerate her proficiency in English and support her overall learning. In addition, Rosa's classroom teacher is keenly aware of the fact that she is an English leaner and tries to provide some adaptations, such as bilingual handouts, to help Rosa access her lessons. However, as the vignette shows, despite these supports, Rosa is facing a number of hurdles in her academic development, which undermine her school learning as well as her belief that she can be a successful student. In what follows, we will identify and briefly discuss some of those hurdles.

Discontinuity Between Mainstream and ESL Class Curricula. A common challenge faced by EBs in pull-out ESL programs is the discontinuity between the curriculum in their mainstream classrooms and the content taught in their ESL classes. Pull-out ESL programs typically have emergent bilingual students like Rosa meeting a set number of hours per week in a class with an ESL teacher and a small group of EBs from different mainstream classrooms to work on improving their English language proficiency. Ideally, Rosa's ESL teacher would be coordinating with her classroom teacher to incorporate content and academic vocabulary from the mainstream classroom into the work EBs do in the ESL class.

But the number of students that Rosa's ESL teacher has to work with every week and the fact that Rosa's group-mates come from different classrooms and grade levels makes this kind of coordination all but impossible—a challenge that is also common in the push-in ESL model. As a result, the ESL teacher follows her own independent curriculum, preparing and teaching lessons that aim to develop her students' English language competence. However, this means that the learning Rosa does in her ESL room does not have many viable connections to what she does in her mainstream class, often seeming like one more subject she needs to work on instead of a support structure that facilitates her overall academic learning.

Instruction Loss. Another challenge that is visible in Rosa's vignette is the loss of instruction that inevitably happens when students are not continuously present in the mainstream classroom. The schedule of pull-out ESL support is tied to the caseload of the ESL teacher, which often means that EB students have to leave their mainstream classrooms in the middle of a lesson and then walk back in the middle of a different one. Even in better situations, when the pull-out sessions are coordinated with the school schedule and EBs travel to and from ESL class during natural breaks in the schedule, the rest of the class is still receiving instruction while the EBs are away in their pull-out ESL group. Missing lessons or parts of lessons can be disruptive for any student, but it becomes even more of a challenge when this loss of instruction occurs frequently and steadily week after week. For example, Rosa is taken out toward the end of the language arts block, so she misses reading and writing time, when students study new vocabulary and literature genres and practice writing skills. This means Rosa misses the meaning-embedded reading and writing opportunities of her language arts class every day.

Taking EBs like Rosa to the ESL room during other subjects, such as science, math, or social studies, is not an ideal solution either, as it means that they consistently miss out on the content from one or more of those subjects while they attend ESL class. This systematic loss of instruction and learning experiences can become quite a burden, particularly in combination with the fact that, when they return to their regular classrooms, emergent bilinguals have to make do with instruction being delivered in a language they do not yet know very well. As a result, the task of staying up to speed with the rest of the class and meeting the learning objectives in a satisfactory manner becomes even more of a challenge.

Interpersonal Versus Academic Language.

Interpersonal Versus Academic Language. Another challenge noted in Rosa's vignette is the difference between interpersonal and academic language and how even students who have been in the United States for a long time may still need additional support in becoming proficient users of the kind of English necessary for school success. Many EBs like Rosa may be quite comfortable chatting with their friends in English and have everyday conversations in a manner that is almost indistinguishable from their native English-speaking peers. However, the English of literature and the specialized vocabulary of the different subject areas of the curriculum are very different and pose a significant challenge for EBs.

In the early 1980s, Jim Cummins (1980, 1981b) introduced the idea that there is a distinction between the English spoken in informal, everyday conversations (Basic Interpersonal Communication Skills [BICS]) and the English spoken in classrooms, which is necessary for success in schools (Cognitive Academic Language Proficiency [CALP]). Indeed, becoming aware of this distinction is a surprise and a relief to many teachers who are baffled and frustrated when they watch their EB students speaking English fluently and confidently on the playground and in the cafeteria, and then struggling when they have to speak or write in the classroom. Not knowing the difference between BICS and CALP can lead teachers to interpret the EBs' behavior in the classroom as the result of inattention, laziness, or insolence, instead of as a natural phenomenon in the process of learning a new language.

Though research over the past years has challenged and refined Cummins's original concepts of BICS and CALP for EBs, the idea that students need to develop academic language proficiency in English in order to be academically successful is still very relevant, and it is a significant principle behind many ESL programs. In the vignette, the key-terms bilingual definition sheet Ms. Meyer gives Rosa as she enters the classroom is an effort to support Rosa's CALP development. Indeed, such vocabulary supports are a highly recommended and very commonly used adaptation for EBs in mainstream classrooms. In addition, many of the lessons Rosa's ESL teacher teaches during their pull-out sessions aim to develop both the communicative and academic vocabulary of EBs and enhance their ability to function in school and society by learning to read and understand different texts. However, as discussed above, with limited time and much to learn in ESL class and in their school days, emergent bilinguals like Rosa often experience these efforts as an assortment of disjointed activities that do not come together as a coherent approach that supports their proficiency in English or their ability to better handle the academic demands of the curriculum.

Overwhelming Verbal Input. A typical lesson in a U.S. classroom involves quite a bit of verbal expression: Teachers talk to provide information, explanations, and instructions, and students talk to respond to questions, discuss issues and topics with peers in their groups, and ask for explanations and clarifications. As shown in the vignette, for Rosa, like other EBs, the highly verbal nature of instruction in most mainstream classrooms can be quite overwhelming. In order to successfully participate in oral conversations, speakers must be able to hear and understand what others are saying. Then they can take a conversation turn to make a contribution that matches the content and the flow of the interaction and helps the conversation move forward. So, for example, when a student hears the class wondering about how many calves a heifer typically has, an appropriate contribution at that point of the interaction would be to respond that cows typically have one baby at a time. Contributing this same piece of information several turns after the class dealt with that question and students are now talking about chickens is not equally effective and may even be dismissed by the other speakers as being off-topic.

To better understand the challenge Rosa and other EBs face when having to contribute to a class discussion, think back to a situation when you found yourself as part of a large, loud, and very talkative group of people discussing a topic (maybe at a Thanksgiving dinner or a lively faculty meeting). How easy was it to keep track of all that was being said and to find the space to contribute your input over your very chatty uncle or the colleague who kept interrupting you? Now consider the same situation, but add to it the extra challenge of everyone else speaking in a language you don't know very well. Under those circumstances, keeping track of information presented orally with insufficient visual or other support can be extremely difficult, particularly when there are few opportunities for you to pre-think or rehearse what you want to say before you have to say it. Indeed, as bilinguals, we can attest that participating in multiperson conversations can be one of the most challenging types of interactions, even for people with a high degree of proficiency in a language. The challenge multiplies for EBs who are learning new concepts in a new language and have to listen to and speak about a topic for which they may not even have the necessary vocabulary in their home language.

Snowball Effect. Toward the end the vignette, we see Rosa put her head down on her desk, frustrated by her inability to stay on top of the lesson happening around her. Even in a situation such as the one captured in the vignette, when Rosa probably knows more about the topic at hand than many of the other class members and she could offer valuable insight to the rest of the class, she cannot find an access point to the class conversation. The discontinuity between the content of her mainstream class and her ESL class, the loss of instruction caused by her travels to and from her pull-out

ESL class, the extra challenge academic language poses for learners, and the highly verbal input of mainstream classrooms can snowball, reaching overwhelming levels for EBs. Despite the special supports put in place by the school, the cumulative effect of these challenges can significantly compromise EBs' ability to access the lessons in their mainstream classrooms and the grade-level content they are expected to master.

Yan, a 2nd-Grader in a Translanguaging Classroom

The vignette that follows shows a promising alternative in a translanguaging classroom that effectively addresses the challenges we observed in Rosa's story.

Fall. Yan arrived in the United States 2 months ago, and this is the 2nd week he is attending his 2nd-grade class. He is the only Chinese person in this class. It is writing workshop time, and all the children around him are quietly writing, bending over their desks, pencils in hand. His teacher, Mrs. Rush, had just finished explaining a writing task, and all of the other students got right to work. Yan, holding a pencil in his hand, is looking around the room wondering what to do. He knows he is supposed to be writing, but what? Mrs. Rush approaches Yan's desk with a Chinese/English bilingual picture book in her hand. She points at the words and pictures in the book and puts a piece of paper on his desk, saying something to Yan. Though he can't understand all of her words, he figures out what Mrs. Rush wants him to do: She wants him to write something just like the book! Using the book and the classroom word walls to support him, he gets to writing. The product of his work is shown in Figure 2.1.

When he shows it to Mrs. Rush, she reads it with a big smile. When she is done, she tells him "good job" and gives him an excited thumbs-up. She even invites him to share his work with the whole class. After his reading and showing his work to the class, he receives a big applause from his classmates who are all impressed by his ability to write in two languages.

Spring. Yan reaches for the green crayon while glancing at Anna's drawing of a bean sprout. Pointing at the spot where the stem meets the ground, he spreads his fingers apart as he moves them downward. "Go under dirt," he says as Anna looks at him quizzically. "Food!" he adds helpfully while repeating the motion. "Oh, the roots! I have to add the roots," Anna says realizing what Yan was trying to tell her. "Yes, roots," Yan repeats and begins to add the English word next to 根 in his own diagram with both Chinese and English captions, while Anna reminds him not to forget the two o's in the word *root*.

Mrs. Rush stops by to check in on their progress. Nodding approvingly, she taps the old book of Chinese herbs Yan has on his desk and asks,

Figure 2.1. Yan's writing during the second week of his study in Mrs. Rush's classroom

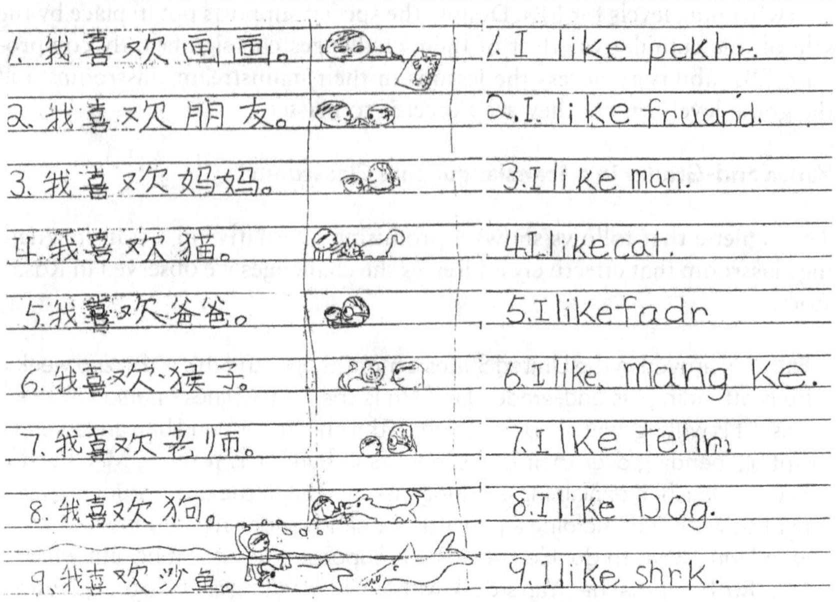

1. 我喜欢画画。	1. I like pekhr.
2. 我喜欢朋友。	2. I like fruand.
3. 我喜欢妈妈。	3. I like man.
4. 我喜欢猫。	4. I like cat.
5. 我喜欢爸爸。	5. I like fadr
6. 我喜欢猴子。	6. I like mang ke.
7. 我喜欢老师。	7. I lke tehr.
8. 我喜欢狗。	8. I like DOg.
9. 我喜欢沙鱼。	9. I like shrk.

"Anything from Grandma Ai on bean sprouts?" "Yes," Yan responds, pointing to a part of his poster written in mixed English and Chinese. "Good for sun," he says, sticking his tongue out and pretending to faint. "Good for a sunstroke?" marvels the teacher. "I need to remember that!"

In these vignettes from a translanguaging classroom, we see a fluid and cohesive learning experience for Yan who speaks Mandarin Chinese with his family, reads and writes in Chinese at a 1st-grade level, has been in the United States for less than a year, and is classified as having *emerging* proficiency in English.

Learning Content Knowledge While Also Developing Language Skills. In the first vignette, we saw Rosa struggle with the fact that the development of her communicative English language skills and the development of her content- and grade-level competencies and relevant academic language were treated as two separate and independent processes, with her ESL teacher being in charge of the former and her classroom teacher of the latter. However, in a translanguaging classroom, communicative and academic language skills are strategically developed right along with the content knowledge and content-specific language of the grade-level curriculum. In the vignette above, we see Yan not simply being allowed, but also encouraged, to use his home language as well as any other tools he possesses to express himself.

In response, he uses written Chinese, written English, and images to create an illustrated bilingual text and participate in a writing workshop just like his peers. In the science class, we see him being supported both by his teacher and his classmates in his English language development, which occurs as a natural part of a lesson on plants. Notably, Yan's use of English does not arise from decontextualized language exercises, but serves as a meaningful contribution to lesson-related interactions with his classmates and with his teacher. In this way, from the very beginning, and though he does not know much English, Yan is able to join the learning community of his classroom as a writer and a learner just like his English-proficient peers, working on practicing his English, developing his academic vocabulary, and building his grade-level content knowledge.

Using All of the Students' Languages in the Service of Learning. Another significant characteristic of translanguaging classrooms is the fact that all of the languages in a student's repertoire are treated as valuable resources and are actively engaged in the service of learning. This is in direct contrast with monolingually oriented approaches, where English is typically the only language used in the process of teaching and learning, and where other languages are, for the most part, unwelcome in the classroom. In the vignette above, Yan learns that writing in Chinese is a legitimate way to respond to the task at hand and does so naturally. He writes in both Chinese and English in the writing workshop, and makes his diagram bilingual in the science class because these representations are helpful in pushing his content mastery forward and in capturing what he knows.

In addition, these bilingual texts make sense because he is interested in expanding his English vocabulary and wants to more effectively communicate with his teacher and classmates who do not know Chinese. Yan also knows that his school is not allowing him to use his home language simply as a crutch until his English is strong enough and he no longer needs it. He is aware the goal is not to forget his heritage tongue. Rather, the school is systematically working to communicate the message that maintaining and developing all of the students' literacies and language proficiencies for the purpose of meaning making are essential goals.

Using Home Language Resources. The goal of supporting all the students' languages and literacies in the classroom is also pursued by utilizing texts and other resources from the students' homes and communities. Of particular usefulness in the learning process for EBs are books in students' home languages that can serve several purposes:

- Provide invaluable information to facilitate content-knowledge development
- Support EBs' continued literacy development in their home language

- Help EBs make connections between concepts in their home
  language and concepts in English

In the fall vignette above, Mrs. Rush uses a bilingual book as a mentor text to encourage Yan to use any languages and tools he has to express himself.

Later in the spring when the class is studying a science unit on plants, Yan brings in Grandma Ai's book on herbs that is written in Chinese, which he keeps on his desk to reference when recording his learning. Indeed, his grandmother is also actively engaged in this unit because Yan told her that his class was learning about bean sprouts and that his teacher always asks him about the herb book. Together Grandma Ai and Yan read the entry on bean sprouts, and she told him a story of how she had used the herb when Yan's mom had a really bad sunstroke when she was little. Although this book is not a leveled textbook that is explicitly tied into grade-level science standards, its impact on Yan's learning experience cannot be understated: Its meaningful inclusion in this lesson encouraged Yan to practice his reading in Chinese, let Yan and his grandmother know that her wisdom and experience are valued by the school, and substantively supported Yan's learning in both content and the English language. It also personalized the learning so Yan connected more deeply to the content.

Casting Students as Experts and Teachers as Co-learners. In monolingually oriented classrooms, standard American English is the only language engaged in the business of school learning, and the teacher is traditionally understood as the only real language expert in the room. Often, this also extends to the teacher being understood as the only content-knowledge expert in the room— the one who already knows what the students are supposed to learn, and the one who judges the correctness and accuracy of what the students say and do. In this context, it is difficult to imagine the students knowing something of value to school learning that the teacher does not already know, or that the students can contribute something to the lesson that the teacher is not able to judge. Rather, the roles are clear-cut and mutually exclusive; teachers are the providers of knowledge and students are the receivers.

However, this order of things cannot stand in a translanguaging classroom where all class members, including the teacher, recognize, embrace, and engage in learning about all of the students' languages and actively use home language resources as part of school learning. In such a context, the students will surely bring in texts and artifacts and use languages the teacher does not know, and they will be able to read, interpret, and compose texts the teacher cannot read. Therefore, there will be situations when the students will wield expertise of language and content that the teacher does not have, and the teacher will rely on the students to use that expertise in productive and helpful ways for themselves and for the rest of the class.

In the vignette about Yan, Mrs. Rush recognizes and honors his bilingual ability and the clever and brave ways in which he expresses himself as a writer. She also acknowledges and draws on his expertise and unique access to the herb book content, an access the teacher herself does not have. Yan's bilingual writing and Grandma Ai's Chinese herb book would have no legitimate place in a traditional classroom. However, in a translanguaging classroom, they cast Yan as a Chinese language expert, and as having content expertise that no one else in the room has. This allows the teacher to shed the sole-expert role of traditional instruction and become a co-learner who stands to be informed by Yan's unique insight and ability.

It is important to note that in shedding the sole-expert role, the teacher does not relinquish the important work of mentoring and guiding students in their learning. Rather, in the writing workshop, Mrs. Rush brings the bilingual book to Yan and encourages him to use it as a model for his own writing. Similarly, in science she references his Grandma Ai's herb book, explicitly encouraging Yan to share his unique knowledge, and acknowledging the value of this knowledge, commenting, "I need to remember that!" The teacher's conduct is not simply a confidence booster for Yan, to make him feel good about himself and his abilities. Most important, the teacher's actions are strategic instructional choices that encourage Yan to use gestures and language for meaningful and effective communication, provide a framework through which he can learn how to own and express his expertise, and model how to be an engaged and proactive learner. As we will discuss in detail in Chapter 4, having teachers shift from an expert role to a co-learner role in translanguaging classrooms can be part of the solution to the bilingual-teacher shortage issue confronting school districts like those in New York and California, where more than 250 languages are spoken among their student population.

Utilizing Collaborative Learning. In the discussion of Rosa's school experiences, we mentioned that the highly verbal nature of mainstream U.S. classrooms can be very challenging for EBs who often have a hard time keeping track of multispeaker conversations and formulating relevant and appropriate contributions at the right time. Though whole-group interactions do have a place in translanguaging classrooms, collaborative learning and opportunities for structured and unstructured interactions with peers are at the heart of the translanguaging model. In the second vignette, Yan is thriving in a collaborative context. When he shared his writing in the writing workshop, his classmates applauded enthusiastically and admired his developing bilingualism, which boosted his self-confidence and facilitated his social integration into his classroom community. In addition, since his teacher encourages students to share their work with one another and exchange feedback for all their written work, Yan has the opportunity to use his English in more intimate, more manageable situations than the formalized and potentially intimidating context of whole-group conversations. In such a setting, Yan feels comfortable in using his first language, his developing English, artwork, and gestures to express himself, without having the pressure of 20-some pairs of impatient eyes looking at him and several mouths eager to say their pieces.

Frequent opportunities for meaningful interactions with a partner or with a small group of peers can offer significant opportunities for emergent bilinguals to practice their oral and written English in a more relaxed context. Indeed, as Collins and Cioè-Peña (2016) state, "in collaborative groups, emergent bilinguals feel empowered in what they know, and are therefore more comfortable appropriating English features into their linguistic repertoires" (p. 134). Collaborative groups can also be a good stage for students to showcase their expertise and home language resources, particularly when they are producing bi- or multilingual texts. And, of course, such interactions can facilitate the development of relationships among the students, ease the enculturation of newcomers to U.S. schools, and help root out the social stigma and isolation issues that often challenge EBs in monolingually oriented classrooms (see Chapter 3).

A caution here, however: Group-work and collaborative learning should not be understood as an easy teaching strategy. A teacher's simply dividing students into groups and telling them to work together can have detrimental effects on the learning of all students, and particularly of EBs. Without a teacher's substantive guidance and support in establishing and practicing group workflows and etiquette, students are likely to flounder. Some students may dominate conversations and decision making, others may be consistently stuck with unwanted tasks, and yet others may fade to the background because they are not able, are not allowed, or do not care to contribute. In the absence of such teacher guidance, group-work can become for EBs an even harder task than whole-group conversations, where at least they can usually count on the teacher to moderate turn-taking and regulate interactions. In poorly run collaborative groups, EBs often have no choice but to withdraw to the background. Therefore, strategically working toward constructing a healthy group-work culture and explicitly teaching students how to work together are vital components of the translanguaging classroom.

Another significant consideration when implementing collaborative learning in the translanguaging classroom is how to group students together. Should teachers group students by ability or create mixed-ability groups? And how about language: Should teachers group children with the same home language together so they can use home language resources to help one another and facilitate their learning? Or should teachers group EBs with native English-speaking students so they are compelled to practice their English? The answer for the translanguaging classroom is that none of these approaches to grouping works best all the time. Rather, the teacher should work toward creating flexible and purposeful groups that are responsive to student needs for any given lesson. In a guide for educators, Celic and Seltzer (2011) advise teachers to be strategic in how they group EBs at various times. Their recommendations include:

- Placing EBs with the same home language in pairs within larger groups so they can have in-depth, sidebar conversations in their home language, and then share their thinking with the rest of their group in English
- Pairing EBs with the same home language but different levels of English proficiency so beginners can be supported in understanding conversations and contributing their own ideas
- Forming groups of three for students with different home languages (one beginner and two students with higher English proficiencies) to avoid newcomer frustration and to be sensitive to the needs of the other two students

CONSIDERING BILINGUAL PROGRAMS OR TRANSLANGUAGING FOR EMERGENT BILINGUALS' ACADEMIC PROGRESS

In the first two vignettes in this section you will see EBs in two kinds of bilingual programs: *dual language bilingual* and *transitional bilingual*. A dual language bilingual program intends to have students with two different native-speaking backgrounds learn two languages together, and aims for them to become proficient and literate in both languages. On the other hand, transitional bilingual programs are designed to have students learn content knowledge in their home language while developing English language proficiency. As their English proficiency develops, more and more content is taught in English until, ultimately, students transition into monolingual mainstream classrooms.

Cata, a 3rd-Grader in a Dual Language Bilingual Program

"Los árboles necesitan oxígeno porque . . ." Cata begins to tell her group before Mr. Saltis interrupts with a reminder that today it's English day in science class. She groans, rolls her eyes, and mutters under her breath, *"Entonces, someone else lo dice."* For the previous class in science, it was Spanish day, and though she was no tree expert, Cata had contributed vigorously. Her family was from Costa Rica and she had spent the first five years of her life in a small town near the rain forest. Bringing in her mom's photos from Costa Rica and sharing them in class had been a highlight. Today, however, she is only supposed to speak in English. Dejected, Cata folds her arms and does not speak another word for the rest of the period.

Jingming, an 8th-Grade Alumnus of a Transitional Bilingual Program

In many ways Jingming is an average teenager who likes hip-hop and fast cars and enjoys hanging out with his friends and playing videogames. He is a pretty good student, though he is definitely much better at math than he is at English. Deep down he hopes to go to college one day because he wants to be an engineer. But half the time he says that he's not sure that he wants to "do the college thing" because he worries that his family cannot afford it and that he won't be a successful college student. Does he really want to put that burden on them?

In most ways, Jingming is a success story. When he first came to the United States 7 years ago, he only knew a handful of English words. Where he lived in New York City, most of his neighbors were also Chinese, and the kids went to the local public school, which had a transitional Chinese and English program. That's where he went too. When he started there as a 2nd-grader, most of his subjects were taught in Chinese. In many ways, it felt as if he had never left China. Alongside this teaching, he and his peers also got intense English language instruction, the teachers reminding them that learning English was their ticket to success in this country. Moving from Chinese to English classes created a whiplash effect as Jingming went from the familiarity of Chinese to everything being about English and the English-speaking world, and then right back again to Chinese. But he persevered. As time went by, Chinese was used less and less in lessons and more and more content was taught in English. Unlike many of his peers who struggled learning English, at the end of 3 years, Jingming was deemed proficient in English. Therefore, he exited the bilingual program and went full-time into regular mainstream education.

And here he is now in 8th grade, still struggling with some English vocabulary and still getting caught off guard with cultural references that mean nothing to him. But he makes do. He is flexible and resourceful—a true engineer. He is still not a good writer, but he figures that engineers do not need writing that much. What really bothers him, though, is that whenever he picks up one of his parents' Chinese books, he feels like a 6-year-old, because he can barely read them. He, who used to be one of the best students in his Chinese class! Jingming, of course, still speaks Chinese with his family, but as Chinese was fading from his school life, reading and writing in Chinese also waned in his out-of-school life, until it was no more.

Concerns About Bilingual Programs

With these two vignettes, we are back inside monolingually oriented classrooms in the context of dual language bilingual and transitional bilingual programs. Although the use of the terms *bilingual* or *dual language* to describe the programs suggests a plurilingual orientation, that is not necessarily the case. In dual language bilingual programs, the intention is the development of bilingualism and biliteracy. However, as we discuss below, the rigid separation of the two target languages that is typical in dual language bilingual programs still reflects a monolingual ideology, as it fails to acknowledge the continuity and simultaneity of individuals' language resources and their mutual effect.

Transitional bilingual programs, which are the most prevalent type of bilingual program in the United States, are also monolingually oriented. Transitional bilingual programs are typically established in areas with high numbers of EBs with the same home language, and are used as a way to help students stay on track with their content knowledge while they are building their English language proficiency. In all, EBs are expected to study for 2–3 years in these programs and then transition into English-only learning settings. To this end, students attending transitional bilingual programs are taught subjects such as math, science, and social studies in their home language and often about their home countries, while receiving intensive instruction in English as a second language. As the students' command of English grows, more and more instruction is delivered in English until eventually the native language is no longer used, and the students exit the program. A major concern about transitional bilingual programs is the absence of any intention to support the maintenance of students' home languages and their literacies in those languages, which often results in literacy loss, as their conception of literacy narrows to only English. As Roberts (1995) notes, "The goals of transitional bilingual education are still assimilationist, and the outcome is generally subtractive bilingualism. Still, it is hoped that these programs will provide the content area support which will enable these students to remain in school" (p. 374).

Below we identify and discuss two concerns that can undermine EBs' academic progress in dual language bilingual and transitional bilingual programs: the incompatibility of school language practices with bilingual instruction and the implicit or explicit privileging of English.

Language Separation as Incompatible with Bilingual Practice. Transitional as well as dual language bilingual programs typically separate languages by assigning a single, specific language to certain subjects and/or certain days and times. The idea behind this practice is that if students are allowed to use whichever language whenever they want, they will choose to use the language in which they are more comfortable and will never get to practice and learn any other languages. We saw this practice in Cata's vignette, when her teacher redirected the students' conversations by reminding them that it was English day. By regulating language use, bilingual programs seek to push students to express themselves in the target language(s) and thus support their proficiency development.

However, note how this practice is based on the assumption of separate linguistic repertoires for each of the languages: On Spanish day you activate your Spanish repertoire, and on English day you turn that one off and activate the English repertoire. As we discussed in the Introduction and Chapter 1, this does not accurately match the ways in which bilinguals use language to think, express themselves, and relate to others. Indeed, studies of bilingual practice suggest that bilinguals use languages flexibly and fluidly to accomplish their communication objectives. When bilinguals engage with the world around them, all their languages are accessed to maximize the effect and efficiency of their communication, thinking, learning, and comprehension.

That is exactly what Cata was attempting to do in her science lesson about the rain forest. Ideally, she should have been able to capitalize on her background knowledge of the rain forest, which was rooted in Spanish, to support her mastery of science curricular objectives and her development of relevant language resources in English. However, the directive of Spanish-only on one day and English-only on the other hindered those connections and compelled Cata to give up on the lesson. Disallowing students to use one of their languages means that they have to artificially force themselves not to use some of their language resources or ways for representing their world, as they are solving a problem, communicating with others, or recording their learning. Forceful separation in language use in our instruction is to limit the bilingual students' ability to learn, to think, and to communicate, and ultimately it suppresses the potential in their learning performance.

Beyond this, we need to remember that translanguaging theory asserts that individuals have a single, unified linguistic repertoire that encompasses all of their language resources, which they strategically deploy as they use language. So, for example, when Xenia is shopping in a U.S. store with her son, she will read the signs in English, speak with her son in both Greek and English, mentally estimate sales prices in Greek, and interact with the cashier in English. These choices are strategic and responsive to her context and to her language toolset: She is able to read and understand the English environmental print around her, she is consciously trying to raise her son to be bilingual, Greek is her "comfort language" in math, and she is aware that English is probably the only common language she has with the cashier.

The ability to make these choices nimbly and effectively is rooted in *sociolinguistic competence*, a key concept in language acquisition which describes individuals' ability to modulate what they say and how they say it in response to different kinds of situations (Hymes, 1974). This is the knowledge that enables us to talk differently to our boss than to a close friend, or that guides us to soften what we say when we are asking for a favor but use firmer language and tone when expressing displeasure. This competence operates in all interactions, and it is significant in helping us communicate effectively. Beginning a text message to a friend with "Dear Ms. Smith" would be taken as a rather odd joke, whereas beginning an email to your boss with "Sup, dude" would probably be seen as quite inappropriate and unprofessional. Knowing what is expected in different communication situations allows us to make strategic choices in how we express ourselves so we can be more effective.

For individuals who speak more than one language or language variety, sociolinguistic competence allows them to read the context of communications and flexibly use the linguistic code or codes that would be most effective in each situation. With this in mind, policing students' language use through arbitrary subject or time constraints seems artificial and potentially counterproductive. How are emergent bilinguals going to learn to make strategic decisions in language choice when they are not given a choice? Rather, it appears that what we should be striving for in education is to help students develop their proficiencies in the different languages of their contexts, hone their ability to make effective strategic choices in the use of their language resources, and critically consider social norms about language use and dominant and marginalized varieties.

Privileging English. A mentioned above, the term *bilingual* in and of itself suggests an equal amount of emphasis to the two languages involved—no hierarchy, no differentiated value. However, in most bilingual programs in the United States there is overt or implied privileging of English. In part, this reflects a pragmatic approach to the U.S. sociocultural context in which standard American English is the dominant variety. It is the main language of instruction in most U.S. educational institutions. English proficiency is required for most high-paying jobs, and participation in mainstream culture is primarily conducted in English. In many other ways, however, privileging English and pushing students toward its rapid acquisition is also ideological. And, in the case of transitional bilingual programs, it comes at the cost of enduring and robust bilingualism and biliteracy. The very notion of transitionality is an embodiment of this ideology since the students' home language has a sanctioned role in their education only as a temporary scaffold, until they acquire enough English to no longer need this support. As in Jingming's case, once students reach a presumably adequate level of English proficiency, the home language is abandoned like a crutch the students no longer need. In the vignette, we saw Jingming's sadness and frustration at the realization that his Chinese literacy was slipping away from him. As we will discuss in Chapter 3, this insidious message of privileging English can have detrimental effects on EBs' identities and on their willingness to learn English or to receive instruction in their home language.

Amira, a 4th-Grade Translanguaging Author

In the vignette that follows, we see how translanguaging practices can offer some promising responses to the challenges outlined above in ways that acknowledge the realities of bilingual lives and strive to prepare students for deliberate and strategic deployment of their language resources.

Amira is writing a personal narrative about going to the ocean for the first time. She has a solid first draft of the story when Ms. Steele approaches her for a student–teacher writing conference. After listening to Amira read her story, Ms. Steele praises her on the level of detail but notes that her story could be improved by the addition of dialogue. "Do you remember our minilesson on dialogue?" she asks. Amira says yes, but seems tentative about the idea. Ms. Steele reminds her that taking others' advice is up to her but asks what is troubling Amira. "Me and my parents spoke in Arabic," she says. "They can't speak to me in English in the story!" "That makes sense," the teacher says. "It makes great sense. Hm . . . We need to see how other authors solved this problem so you can get ideas for your own writing. Remember **Abuela** [Dorros, 1997]?" Amira nods, and catching on, she adds, "and *I Love Saturdays y domingos* [Ada & Savadier, 2004]." "Exactly," says Ms. Steele with a thumbs-up. "I'll get a lesson ready." And handing a Post-it notepad to Amira, she adds, "If you think of any other books . . ."

After Ms. Steele walks away, Amira thinks back to that day when she and her family went to the beach for the first time after moving to the United States. She remembers her dad's anxiety driving along unknown roads, following Siri's instructions; the kids in the back seat chattering in excitement in Arabic and English; her mom kneeling on the beach, sand running through her fingers, whispering a poem in Arabic. As the sun was setting, they all sat in the sand and listened to their parents tell stories from the old country, the Arabic rolling from their minds and off their tongues.

Thumbing through the two books Ms. Steele quietly set on her desk a few minutes after their chat, Amira notes how they include both English and Spanish, which makes them seem more true to life. Amira begins adding dialogue to her story, writing some of the utterances in Arabic and providing explanations in English. Later, during library time she hunts for more bilingual books.

The next day Amira approches her teacher with an armload of bilingual books, pages marked with Post-it notes. "I found some good ones in the library," she says and talks to the teacher about what she noticed. Two days later, Amira helps the teacher teach a lesson on how authors render bilingual characters when writing a story, focusing on character authenticity and reader comprehension.

The Realities of Bilingual Practice. As previously discussed, many ESL programs currently in use in U.S. schools are exclusively focused on developing EBs' English proficiency and literacy. Home languages are often unwelcome in schools, and when they are allowed in the classroom, their presence is typically the result of tolerance rather than of their purposeful and intentional harnessing in the service of learning. Even in bilingual education classrooms, the language used in any particular lesson on any particular subject is often predecided and explicitly regulated. Such practices are incompatible with bilingual realities and deprive students of the opportunity to use all the language resources at their disposal.

In contrast, teachers in translanguaging classrooms, regardless of whether they are in English-dominant or bilingual schools, seek to create educational experiences that are reflective of the affordances and challenges of bilingual lives. In translanguaging classrooms, restrictions in language use do not come from arbitrary guidelines but from having to communicate with specific audiences for specific purposes and in specific situations, evidenced in the following examples:

- In math class, Rodrigo writes notes in Spanish with some English terminology for three reasons: (1) He writes faster in Spanish; (2) it helps him connect this new information to the math he did last year in Mexico City; and (3) he is the only audience/reader for these notes.
- In science class, Adala uses her notes in Urdu and Google Translate to work with her lab mate, a monolingual English-speaking student, on preparing a PowerPoint in English for their presentation to classmates who do not speak Urdu.

In encouraging this kind of decision making, teachers and students inevitably have to contend with the kinds of very real tensions bilinguals grapple with in their daily lives, which involve using all the language resources they have for maximum productivity and effect, and making strategic decisions about how to communicate and through which language(s).

In the vignette about Amira, she struggled with one such tension: maintaining character authenticity (and honoring her own identity as a bilingual Syrian American) and being understood by an English-speaking reading audience. Amira's original hasty solution was to write in English and hide her home language by excluding dialogue from her story. However, Ms. Steele's invitation for exploring solutions other bilinguals have employed allowed Amira to take the challenge on and investigate effective alternatives so she could make an informed, strategic decision and come up with a more elegant solution.

Metacognitive Awareness of Language Choices. By removing arbitrary rules that dictate when to use each language, bilingual students have language choices to make. The sociolinguistic competence they have already developed will help them choose. However, school can help EBs become even better at making these choices by teaching them how to think through the options they have available to them and how to choose the language tools that can be most effective in each situation. Let's imagine an EB student who wants to take notes in science class to use as a resource for writing a lab report in English. The teacher can invite the student to try out different language options (home language, English, various code-mixing options) and reflect on which approach seems to be working better:

- Which way is faster?
- Which way produces notes that are more meaningful and helpful to the student?
- What kinds of notes would be most effective in helping the student write the lab report?
- What if the student is working with others? Does that make a difference?

By encouraging students to experiment with and consider different options, teachers can help EBs become *metacognitively aware* of the choices they have available to them and of the potential implications of using those choices.

In the vignette above, Amira struggled with the decision of how to write about her Syrian family in a story written in English. Ms. Steele did not provide a ready-made solution, but instead encouraged Amira to become a co-expert with her by exploring how others have dealt with the same conundrum, carefully examining the nature and effect of those solutions (What did these bilingual authors do? How did that decision influence the feel of their stories?). Engaging in such metacognitive reflections can be a powerful learning activity, as it can help expand students' sociolinguistic knowledge and allow them to make their own strategic decisions in the future, while also honing the research skills necessary for engaging in similar inquiries independently.

Use of Mentor Texts. When acknowledging students' bilingual lives and purposefully working with them to expand their repertoire as effective communicators, it is important to show EBs that they are members of a vast community of people who are in constant exploration of how to be effective bilinguals. As such, the students can count on many accomplished role models who can offer them ideas for potential solutions to challenges they are facing. In addition, by understanding themselves as members of this community, EBs also realize that they too can participate in its conversations by contributing their own ideas, critiques, and solutions. In Yan's writing class vignette, we see his teacher showing him a bilingual picture book as a mentor text for his writing. In Amira's writing class, we see Amira's teacher introducing her to the idea of tapping mentors all around her for exploring potential solutions to the problem of authentically representing speakers of Arabic in a story for English-speaking audiences without compromising readability. Since Amira is writing a narrative, the natural models for her inquiry were authors of narratives with bilingual speakers.

The mentor texts allowed Yan and Amira to enter into a significant conversation in the community of bilinguals, learn from the solutions of others, and become experts with knowledge to share with the rest of their classes.

CONCLUSION

In this chapter we have portrayed and discussed the academic challenges EBs are facing in ESL, mainstream, and bilingual classrooms, and illustrated with examples how translanguaging can be an approach to tackle these challenges. Rather than treating their languages as separate entities and policing their use, translanguaging practices include all languages EBs have as learning resources and encourage students to use any of these languages to learn, explore, and expand their potential to develop content knowledge while learning a new language.

Translanguaging is a model that can be adopted in any educational settings for EBs. It positions teachers as co-learners, gives equal value to all languages students possess, encourages collaboration among students, and highlights students as language, culture, and content experts. By doing so, translanguaging enables EBs to study new content knowledge and develop academic language along with their English proficient peers and participate in the academic activities at their grade level. Even though translanguaging cannot be the only solution to deal with all issues and challenges our EBs face academically in their learning, the practice is an approach to activate the language resources EBs bring with them and use them in the service of their learning.

By encouraging students to utilize all their language resources, EBs can feel empowered to describe the world as they experience it, using the languages of their memories, of their homes, and of the world around them. In the next chapter, we will discuss how translanguaging can be used as an approach to deal with social challenges emergent bilinguals face in the school environment.

CHAPTER 3

Meeting Social Challenges

In Chapter 2 we discussed the academic challenges emergent bilingual students encounter in monolingually oriented classrooms and argued that translanguaging pedagogy offers a promising alternative. In addition to academic hardships, EB students in educational contexts that focus on monolingualism also face social challenges. In the English-speaking, majority-culture context of most U.S. schools, emergent bilinguals are on the outside in many regards: racially, ethnically, culturally, and linguistically. Yet the school years are critical for young people's development of social bonds and savviness by becoming enculturated in the norms, expectations, relational skills, and etiquette of society.

Unfortunately, many of the special programs currently in place to support EBs in U.S. schools are not designed to support this enculturation process. In fact, it can be argued that some basic structural aspects of such programs work against it by separating out emergent bilinguals for instruction, as well as by focusing only on English language acquisition, instead of embracing cultural and language plurality. This affects EBs' experience not only on the playground or in school social events, but also in the classroom where they often feel isolated. They may not have opportunities or be able to participate in group-work, collaborate with classmates on projects, or integrate into the classroom community. Without these necessary skills, their transition to mature life is hampered.

Scarcity of significant opportunities to participate in the school community or to interact with mainstream peers can be problematic for the socialization of EBs. The language barrier, in combination with the stigma often attached to "broken English" or speaking English with a nonnative accent, impacts EBs' chances of building and maintaining successful relationships with their mainstream peers as well as forming robust and well-socialized peer-group identities that comfortably fit in the social world of school. Instead, EBs can feel isolated and are often pushed to join marginalized social groups or even antisocial groups such as gangs. Without strong memberships into mainstream social groups, EBs are forever branded by peers and by themselves as "the other," which may lead to the development of a permanent foreigner identity. This can have disastrous consequences on the future prospects of these individuals, as this marginalization is likely to deprive them of opportunities to hone social skills valued in professional settings. Marginalization can then follow them into their adulthood and can short-circuit their opportunity for socioeconomic or social success.

Beyond the socialization challenges that arise when EBs do not have substantial opportunities to learn as fully integrated members of their school community are the issues that stem from grouping all EB students together, assuming that they share a common identity and have similar learning needs. Based on current structures in U.S. schools, EBs are frequently grouped for ESL services based on their scores on English language proficiency tests. However, as discussed in Chapter 1, not all EBs are the same: They may come from different cultures and ethnic groups; they may have originated from different parts of the world; they may speak different languages; and they may have had different life and educational experiences. Therefore, treating EBs as a monolithic group with minimal, if any, attention to their individual stories, experiences, and knowledge can be quite problematic for their social development. Though students in an ESL classroom are apt to share the same status of limited proficiency in English, they may share little else.

The language we speak shapes not only our cultural identities, but also our social identities, our sense of belonging. When EBs, even those born in the United States, cannot share their heritage tongues in school, there may also be social isolation and withdrawal. Ultimately, school personnel must work toward creating a welcoming environment that is ready and willing to help build strong relationships with EBs and their families, and create opportunities for them to meaningfully interact and collaborate with a wide variety of teachers and peer groups, and become full participants in the school community.

In the first part of this chapter, we share three stories of EBs from different backgrounds in monolingually oriented learning situations to illustrate the social challenges they encounter in classes and schools. Then, in contrast, we present three examples of EBs in translanguaging environments to show how they are recognized and accepted into the school community as bi/multilingual individuals and learners.

EMERGENT BILINGUALS IN MONOLINGUAL SCHOOL SETTINGS: ENCOUNTERING SOCIAL CHALLENGES

Emergent bilinguals, whether U.S.- or foreign-born, often are not aware of all the cultural norms of so-called mainstream American culture, and do not know what is considered acceptable behavior in certain settings. When can one bend the rules, and when should one follow them explicitly? Their lack of awareness of the social norms may make EBs especially cautious about stepping on the toes of others or may cause them to apologize profusely. They may internalize and take personally a lot of the negative reactions of individual peers, assuming that they represent how they are perceived in the eyes of the entire majority culture, instead of brushing them off as the whims of specific individuals. Now, let us consider from a social perspective the stories of three EBs.

Maria: A U.S.-Born Emergent Bilingual

Emergent bilinguals are often thought of as recent immigrants, but in reality, over half of the EB students in U.S. schools were born in this country, and many are the children of first-generation immigrants. Though they are natural-born citizens of the United States, they often do not feel natural in the country of their birth and the only nation in which they have ever lived. U.S.-born EBs often grow up in insular immigrant communities where they hear a lot about their parents' home countries, speak their heritage language, and experience the cultural traditions of their parents' homeland. When they step out of their homes and communities, however, they sense an otherness in the mainstream society. At schools, due to their limited proficiency in English, they are labeled as ELs just like those who are newly arrived in this country.

U.S.-born EBs find themselves between two worlds: the country where they were born and the country of their parents, of which they often have only heard. Yet, they do not feel like they belong to either. Their cultural identification can be fluid and conflicted, pulled in two different ways of knowing and naming the world. With the language differences, the way in which they interact with the world is different as well. It is as if two definitions contend for legitimacy in their world. These individuals often live their lives between two social realities, between two social norms. To illustrate this tension, we share the story of Maria, a U.S.-born Mexican American girl.

Maria is a 10-year-old 4th-grader. Though Maria was born in the United States and has never set foot inside Mexico, her first language is Spanish, which is spoken in her home and community. At school, she does not really have many friends and prefers to either sit by herself or with other Mexican American classmates. Her parents are undocumented; her mother had crossed the border pregnant with her 11 years ago. Today, they live tucked away from view in a wooded patch of one-story tenements.

Throughout her childhood, Spanish has been the language of her home and neighborhood, where legends and folklore were given breath, and English became the language of school, where academic learning took place. Prior to 1st grade, Maria had attended a community school taught by parents from her neighborhood and volunteers from the local university. But her parents sent her to the local public school because they wanted her to socialize more with mainstream peers. In her current school, Maria spends an hour a day out of her mainstream classroom to study with other EBs identified as English learners. When she gets up to leave for ESL class, she feels very self-conscious as she creeps out of the room as quietly as possible. She feels like she is being sent to a different school inside the school, singled out as needing special assistance. Coming from her two worlds of a Spanish-speaking home and an English-speaking school, she feels that her school world is also split into two separate worlds: that of her ESL classroom and that of her mainstream class.

This trek is repeated daily and her social life suffers for it. The only common time she has with the students from her ESL group is that 1 hour a day in the ESL room. Though she has become friendly with some of them, Maria often feels that the only thing she has in common with many of them is that they are all learning English. On the other hand, she does not feel like a full member of her regular classroom either. Every time she walks back in, her classmates are doing something different, and Maria feels left out. Often, the teacher will come to her seat, and try to explain to her what everyone else was doing. This makes her feel even more different from her peers.

Solidifying friendships through after-school activities is not really an option either. Maria's family is counting on her for household chores and looking after her younger brothers, so she always comes straight home after school, never able to participate in after-school programs or attend social gatherings. Her friends are other Mexican American peers in her neighborhood. The few friends she does have at school are other bilingual Mexican American girls. So, when she engages with her friends, she typically speaks a mixture of Spanish and English. When she started school, she did not know any English, but thanks to interactions with her classmates and teachers, including her ESL instructor, she is learning to engage with her world using the English language, which has now become easier for her. Yet she still cannot pass the English proficiency test and is in danger of being labeled as a "long-term EL."

In her mainstream class Maria seems to shy away from her English-speaking classmates. Ms. Hale, her 4th-grade teacher, often assigns group-work, but in these groups Maria mostly stays quiet and lets the other members do all the work. She also tries to avoid speaking up in class or reading her work out loud, although that is not always possible, as the following vignette shows:

Before Halloween, Ms. Hale gives everyone the assignment of sharing a ghost story. Maria immediately thinks of the legend of La Llorona, the story of the ghostly woman who searched for her slain children in the darkness of the lake in which they drowned. The night her mom first told Maria and her sisters the story, she could not even fall asleep. In class, as soon as she starts thinking of what to write, however, her excitement dissipates. How would she say *"la Llorona"* in English? How would she capture in English the desperation and eeriness of *"Ay, mis hijos!"* in her ghostly cries? And would her classmates find it as scary as she and her sisters did or would they laugh at this old folksy story? Giving up trying to compose her story in English, Maria takes a fresh sheet of paper and begins planning a made-up story about a vampire. While she is planning it, she feels like she is just cobbling together all of the vampire stories she has heard or seen on television.

Later, as she stammers to read her story aloud in class, she sees that Barbara is rolling her eyes, Jessie has his head inside his arms folded on his desk, and Andy is reading his comic book hidden under his seat. Maria feels that her story is not given the same attention as those of her peers, but she doesn't know whether her English reading is incomprehensible or her story is just not interesting. She feels disconnected in this class community and questions her place in the country of her birth.

The languages in Maria's life affect her sense of comfort and belongingness. When asked why she does not socialize with dominant-culture peers, she replied, "Sometimes I feel they just don't understand me. It's mostly because they don't speak my language." In explaining this statement further, it became clear that Maria was not just talking about her peers being unable to understand the Spanish words, but also the cultural and experiential meanings that are part of her life as a Mexican American. As a result, most of Maria's friends are other EBs of Mexican heritage. Much like many other American-born EBs, Maria finds it difficult to immerse into majority-culture peer social circles.

Desperate to fit into the mainstream social circles, Maria tries to conform to peer customs and norms, religiously listening to Ariana Grande and Katy Perry on the radio. Yet, regardless of how much cultural savvy she can manage, her native language and nonmainstream cultural experiences seem to build a wall, separating her from mainstream peers. As she walks through the halls during school, the English-only conversations she overhears almost act as a barrier for social access, as if they are constructing a reality that is off-limits. Languages and dialects do not simply exist in books, but they live on the lips and in the minds of their speakers. When the members of a community share a language, they bond over shared meanings and understanding, which develops a social kinship. Language imparts a collective identity, a collective way of naming the world and branding feelings.

Sometimes, the "same" words have different meanings in different linguistic and cultural contexts. For example, when discussing her mother's crossing from Mexico, Maria referred to the "border" as *la frontera*, but *la frontera* also means "frontier." So, the border when spoken of in English or Spanish can have nuanced distinctions in meaning and tone. These distinctions in how language crosses linguistic boundaries affect the ease with which speakers of those languages negotiate their world.

In a monolingually oriented school, there is also *la frontera* between the languages and social realities of Maria's life. This *frontera* in Maria's social life limits her interactions to only other Mexican American EBs like her, which prevents her from authentic engagements with majority-culture peers. It is no wonder all of her friends are like her, because the linguistic and cultural border has also conjured a social border. These borders may all serve the same purpose as the national border: to protect one's own space from invasion by an unknown other. But, just as *la frontera* can also mean a "frontier," this bordered space of languages can herald new life possibilities if emergent bilinguals are supported in constructing robust identities as bilinguals, with the capacity to negotiate and successfully transcend linguistic and social *frontera*s, without having to forsake their belongingness to either side of the border.

Chien: A Foreign-Born Emergent Bilingual

Foreign-born EB students who come to U.S. schools have left their familiar friends, teachers, and memories for an entirely new life context. In their new classrooms, they must learn to speak, read, and write in a different language than they had been accustomed to and build new social circles.

This new beginning is daunting for these students, who have left behind much of their past experiences in their countries of origin for an unknown future in a place where they sometimes feel unwelcomed. They do not understand U.S. norms and customs and often struggle to decipher others' reactions or expressions. They are hesitant to engage with others for fear of upsetting some social norm they do not understand. They have left behind their familiar social network of community and familial support for a tentative situation in their new homes. Whereas they had imagined their family happily enjoying the many blessings of American modern life, they often find that their parents have to work long hours and that their life is mostly spent struggling in school in the early part of the day and feeling lonely at home in its latter part. To illustrate the experience of many foreign-born emergent bilinguals in U.S. schools, we present the story of Chien, a 16-year-old boy who moved to Texas from Vietnam 2 years ago.

Chien lives in a one-room apartment in an urban setting with his mom, who works at a laundromat. They live sparingly and count every penny. So, no brand-name clothes, no eating out, and no extracurricular activities. Chien was in the 8th grade when he left Vietnam for the United States, but since arriving here, he was put in English-only classes, which he has been failing. This is now his second time in the 8th grade, so he knows his teachers well. One tried to joke with him at the start of the new school year. "You again?" he had said. "You must have really liked my class." Chien did not think it was funny.

The teacher in his English class never calls on him because she does not want to embarrass him in front of his peers. She just assumes that he does not know the answer or that he has never studied the subject back home.

But Chien would like to contribute, if only he had time to respond and his classmates were patient enough to hear him out. On his papers, his teachers often write comments like "Need to review grammar rules" or ask "Did you understand the assignment?"

When he looked around his classrooms at the beginning of the year, there was a sea of new faces, new people he had to meet and try to make friends with. Although he has tried initiating conversations with his peers, they seem to go nowhere. "I'm gonna have new ones next year," he sighs, "so, why bother?" As far as he is concerned, every year everything would just repeat. He would be in a new class, in the same grade, with the same experiences. On their end, afraid to be associated with a problem student, most classmates steer clear of him.

Given that he has already been here for 2 years, Chien has almost given up on trying to fit in. He instead just tries to keep up through his Facebook page with his old friends in Vietnam, where he had been a popular guy. He had many friends, and weekends meant hopping from one house to the next in search of parties and get-togethers. With such warmth tied to his old life, he does not want to let go of that old comfort, including the Vietnamese language. English, on the other hand, has none of the same appeal. English, to him, is cold and lonesome, something he does not truly desire. At home, Chien's favorite pastime is watching YouTube videos of the Vietnamese sitcom, *Cheerful Singles*. He feels most comfortable watching Vietnamese programs.

In his previous school, Vietnamese language and literature had been Chien's best subject, and he had read his favorite book, *Ticket to Childhood* by Nguyen Nhat Anh (2014), more times than he could count. That was a story about a man looking back at his childhood, an activity Chien now does regularly.

As he sits in that now familiar 8th-grade homeroom with the beige cracked paint peeling away from the windows, Chien struggles to understand the teacher. By now, he has grown accustomed to the curriculum, which is the same as last year. Even with help from his ESL teacher, who sometimes attends class with him, he has trouble understanding the specific details he needs to remember for tests. His ESL teacher does not speak Vietnamese, so she tries to explain the lessons using simplified English. Vietnamese is never invited in. Sitting alone in his mainstream class with the push-in ESL teacher in the corner, reading simplified English books, he feels like he is being nudged back into elementary school. When asked, he complains, "The rest of them are reading real texts in real books and I'm stuck with kid stuff. It's embarrassing."

For writing, his ESL teacher taught Chien how to use simple language to express his thoughts in English so he can demonstrate what he knows. But Chien regrets that he cannot express in English the personalized details that gave his writing in Vietnamese its essence. He has to simplify and dilute his thoughts so they fit with the simple English words he knows.

Isolation from the New World. Much like Maria in the previous section, Chien does not feel that he fits in the mainstream classroom, but he also does not like being taken out every day for ESL class either. In that class he is grouped with several other "foreign students" and is treated as if he needs remedial help to reach the same level of achievement as his native-speaking classmates. Back in Vietnam he was one of the best students in his class, and now he is stuck filling in grammar worksheets and struggling to make sense of his lessons' content in English. His peers know him as "the ESL kid" and see him as faulty or relegate his in-class contributions to token comments not to be truly taken seriously or on par with the comments of others.

As suggested in Maria's case as well, being taken out of class can be socially awkward for students. Especially in middle school, when conformity with the peer group is important, distinguishing EBs as such by excluding them from mainstream courses for remedial English instruction may lead to lower self-esteem and a sense of shame in the scrutiny of peers. This is particularly pronounced in the case of immigrant youth; because they have left so much of their social network behind in their home countries, these students are especially sensitive to feeling excluded. Moving to a new school can be a rough transition for any teenager. However, when the language barrier and unfamiliarity with the mainstream culture are added to the mix, social bonding and full immersion in social peer groups can become particularly daunting.

Alienation. For students like Chien, there is a chasm between their former social identities and their current ones. In the present mainstream U.S. context, these students may feel cut off from the social hub, and as a result feel a sense of alienation. Though he has been living in the United States for almost 2 years, to Chien, the real world is still the one portrayed in his favorite Vietnamese television shows and the online world of his friends. Against his hopes when he first moved here, his current environment does not appeal to him. At lunch, Chien usually sits in the corner by himself, reading a Vietnamese comic book while eating the food he made the night before. He sits as far from other students as he can, because he saw a girl make a face as he opened up his lunch box the first day of class. The unfriendly or weirded-out looks he gets from classmates make him feel unwelcomed and excluded. Once on the bus ride back home, one boy even yelled at him from the back of the bus, "Go back to China, bro!" Such negative encounters do not happen every day, and not everyone is guilty of them, but they are common enough to influence the way Chien understands his position among his peers and in this country, and have squelched his willingness to try to engage with his peers around him.

Foreign-born EBs often find it difficult to build meaningful social relationships with others, and consistently view themselves as distinct from established social circles in and out of school. As evidenced in the example above, non-EB peers may use anti-immigrant rhetoric and derogatory language to intimidate or marginalize EBs regardless of whether they are recent immigrants like Chien or they were born in this country like Maria. Even more frequently, though, emergent bilinguals encounter both purposeful and unconscious microaggressions like being excluded from social groups or treated as not having the capacity to learn. Among such aggressions is the tendency to lump all people with a certain accent or some general physical characteristics into the same group regardless of their actual backgrounds. In this way, all people who look Asian are assumed to be Chinese and everyone who speaks Spanish or has a Latin accent is assumed to be Mexican.

Marginalization. EB students often face isolation in schools, as they are stripped of the familiar context they had been accustomed to, as shown in Maria's and Chien's stories above. Aside from the purely linguistic challenges, there are also many sociocultural practices and nuances they must learn, such as saying "excuse me" after burping or when brushing against someone, or how to abide by American expectations regarding people's personal space. EBs' social competences are often developed in cultural contexts of a different country or of a U.S.-based immigrant community, and they do not always match the social expectations of mainstream American culture.

Conversely, many majority-culture individuals blame any seemingly uncouth actions of EB students on a perceived lack of intelligence, poor upbringing, or character flaws. Because they themselves acquired social competence in the majority culture by growing up in it, they are not consciously aware of the intricacies of cultural norms or of the fact that the ways, practices, and expectations of their own culture are neither universal nor more valid than the practices of other cultural groups. As a result, majority-culture individuals often do not excuse the missteps of EBs as part of a learning process.

Emmanuel: The Social Struggles of a Success Story

In the stories above, we introduced emergent bilinguals who are not yet comfortably proficient in English, and discussed the social challenges they encounter in monolingually oriented education settings. Separating EBs from their mainstream peers for instruction impedes their developing strong peer relationships and creates a *frontera* that hampers mutual understanding. We also pointed out how the push for all school learning to happen through English discourages EBs from using all their language resources to support their learning and denies them the opportunity to show what they know without being restrained by their proficiency in English. It also deprives them of the opportunity to explore what it means to be an accomplished bilingual in the world, linguistically, emotionally, and socially. As a result, their social positioning as knowledgeable individuals who have something to offer suffers, and alienation, isolation, and marginalization ensue.

As we noted above, these struggles can deprive young EBs of significant opportunities to develop the social knowledge and intercultural savvy often associated with socioeconomic success. However, these struggles can be seen as less important if we think that they are only relevant to individuals who are still emergent as bilinguals and that their significance will simply dissipate as EBs' English gets stronger. Below, we share the story of an experienced bilingual to help illustrate that social struggles are also part of the experience of the "success stories" of monolingually oriented education.

Emmanuel was born in Cote d'Ivoire, or the Ivory Coast, where his family spoke Dyula and also French, which is the country's official language. His family could afford to send Emmanuel to a private French language school. His parents had gone to college in France but also knew English fairly well. When Emmanuel was 8 and his sister was 5, his parents moved the family to the United States, following his father who got a job at a U.S. tech company based in Connecticut. Their family is fairly well-off financially and can enjoy the comforts of an upscale house in a pricey neighborhood. Once they became U.S. citizens, they were even able to bring his mom's parents to the United States, and get them settled into a condo near their house.

When Emmanuel started school in the United States, he was determined to learn English, fit in, and be a good student. Though the experience was bewildering, with the help of his teachers at school, the tutors his parents hired, and through interactions with a couple of neighboring families who became close friends, Emmanuel's English flourished. By the end of elementary school, a casual observer could not even tell that English was not Emmanuel's first language. Now, as an 8th-grader, Emmanuel does well academically, and he and his parents are already talking about college and future careers. He also appears to be very well adjusted socially: He has a solid group of good friends with whom he hangs out in and out of school, and has even more friendly acquaintances; he is a member of his school's basketball team as the starting shooting guard.

At home, Emmanuel and his family speak a mixture of Dyula, French, and English. He is very close to his grandparents and is friendly with other Ivorians he met though Ivorian socials and cultural events. Indeed, his parents are very involved in the small Ivorian community in their area and expect both their children to stay connected to their heritage and participate in such events. But Emmanuel is rather embarrassed to admit that he tries hard to keep his two worlds apart. Wherever he is, he tries his best to fit in and blend in. At home, he is a dutiful Ivorian son and grandson, but at school and out in mainstream society, he tries to be as American as possible. He worked very hard to get rid of his accent and to eliminate all Ivorian mannerisms from his behavior when interacting with mainstream people. He always buys lunch to avoid "ethnic-looking" home lunches, and he never invites school friends to the house. "If they knew the real me, they'd probably think that my family and I are weird," he says. "And my parents would probably think my friends are too loud and rude. It's best to keep them separate."

At this point, his Ivorian background rarely comes up at school and Emmanuel avoids making any references or connections that would bring attention to himself as an immigrant, a foreigner, or a bilingual. In fact, he is pretty sure that his teachers are not even aware that he speaks another language at home or that his country of origin is Cote d'Ivoire. They just think he is African American. "That works just fine with me," Emmanuel says. Though in the next breath he adds, "It's tiring, though. I feel like I'm always putting on a show—switching masks: to be an Ivorian at home and your average American teenager at school."

From the perspective of a monolingually oriented educational system, Emmanuel is a wonderful success story. Within a few years of being in an American school, he became proficient in the English language, was able to engage in healthy academic performance, and is now college bound. And indeed, on the surface Emmanuel is well adjusted and successful and is able to match his behavior to the expectations of both his home and school communities. However, the sadness and struggle he expresses when he says that he feels like he is constantly putting on a show should be very concerning. What to the outside world appears to be a well-adjusted, positively socialized young man, from the perspective of Emmanuel himself is a person who is constantly hiding significant parts of himself. This split that Emmanuel forced upon himself in order to become the success story the outside world sees and celebrates does not allow him to construct an integrated, confident identity. Rather, he is constantly vigilant about being "outed" as an immigrant and a foreigner at school, well aware of the associated stereotypes and preconceptions.

Opportunities Lost to EBs and to the Mainstream School Community

Maria and Chien feel isolated and marginalized because of their identities as emergent bilinguals. When always seen by others as on the fringe of school or society in general, these students may have trouble in feeling good about themselves or about their place in the United States. Their social identities and activities remain on the margins, never really seen or valued by the school. Emmanuel tried to avoid this pitfall by hiding his heritage background. However, his school and mainstream peers only see and value the mainstreamed part of Emmanuel—a mirror he holds up to show them their own reflection. The other part of Emmanuel's identity, the different part, is just as unseen and marginalized as that of Maria and Chien.

Young people like Emmanuel, as well as Maria and Chien, have significant language and cultural knowledge that is outside of the experience of the American mainstream. By failing to recognize their knowledge and enable EBs to productively participate in the learning process, the school misses out on the full contributions of these students. Classmates and teachers miss out on learning about their stories, learning about the unique realities these students know. Thus, the marginalization of these students also disadvantages the mainstream community.

Students like Maria, Chien, and Emmanuel experience significant discontinuity between their lives at home and their lives at school—different languages, different cultures, different expectations. As they develop friendships and make acquaintances in the U.S. context, they see their world as defined and partitioned by the different languages that exist in each arena. Their social worlds are kept separate as a consequence.

These youths struggle to fit in; to be accepted by their peers, they have to change how they speak and behave. Their social worlds, as with any age group, are an important aspect of their identities. But, especially during the critical stages of childhood and adolescence, when our most enduring memories and lessons regarding social protocol and interactions are formed, these youths need to be able to interact candidly with their world. Translanguaging, either in speech or text, can serve as a means to articulate their candor. In the following section we will present how, through translanguaging, emergent and experienced bilinguals can utilize their home languages and cultures as segue to both language acquisition and social development.

TRANSLANGUAGING AS AN ALTERNATIVE SOCIAL OUTLOOK AND LEARNING ENVIRONMENT

The social marginalization of EBs may be partially connected to their linguistic identity (Blackledge & Creese, 2010; Gunderson, 2007). As we have pointed out, they often live in cultural and linguistic enclaves in which many residents share a common language other than English. Through their experiences in their neighborhoods, EBs often learn to view, name, understand, and interact with the world through their home languages and through the norms and values of their home communities. In monolingually oriented educational settings, these languages and understandings stay outside of school, and a different language and different ways of understanding the world are promoted and privileged.

As we illustrated in the first part of the chapter, such monolingual orientations to education can create significant barriers to the social development and social adjustment of emergent and experienced bilingual children. By limiting the formal world of school to English, students who speak languages other than English are compelled to separate their home and school lives and often have a hard time finding comfortable memberships in diverse groups within their school community. In contrast, translanguaging stands to bridge the social divides between EBs' families and communities and the English-based, dominant-culture context of the larger society by encouraging students to use all their language resources as part of their schoolwork and by purposefully engaging English learners as bilinguals-in-the-making.

When EB students are immersed in a translanguaging context, where different languages can come together to make meaning, their views of the world and themselves acquire a sense of multiplicity, and they learn to see themselves as having different but congruent identities in different contexts. However, in monolingual contexts where English is privileged, the students who are found to be not proficient in English are labeled as deficient, with the many academic and social consequences previously discussed. In a translanguaging context, emergent bilinguals are positioned as skilled communicators of diverse languages and experts of their home languages and cultures. This reframing of their identity could have benefits for their self-image, confidence, and socialization.

A shift in emergent bilinguals' self-image brings about benefits for interpersonal relationships. Whereas before they may have gravitated toward speakers of their first language, now, in a translanguaging classroom, one language is not prioritized over another, and all languages and language-speakers are treated with the same respect and admiration, and have ample opportunities to work and talk with one another under those circumstances. EBs are not confined to social circles dictated by language fluency, but can venture into any context where interests coincide. This is also an analogy for translanguaging itself. No language is privileged over another, and meaning and connections are the most important factors. In this scenario, emergent bilinguals can weave in and out of social circles, recognized for their linguistic and cultural capitals, as we illustrate with the following stories of three EBs.

Revisiting Maria: Expressing and Sharing a Bilingual Self

As we discussed in Chapter 2, giving students the opportunity to bring all their languages and spheres of understanding together can yield some powerful thinking and unique and sophisticated understandings that would not have been possible otherwise. In turn, sharing that thinking with others can help EBs create positive social positions in which they are understood as bilingual, bicultural individuals with unique perspectives and contributions that are valuable to all their communities.

To illustrate this, we are revisiting Maria, the U.S.-born Mexican American girl we met earlier in the chapter. This story takes place 3 years later when, in 7th grade, she decided to take a Spanish class.

Maria made the choice to enroll in Spanish because she wants to be a translator in the future to help people like her parents survive in the United States. She is in a class with other Spanish speakers, and beginning to learn to read and write in Spanish. Although she could always speak Spanish, it was not until she began formally studying the language that she began writing in Spanish.

Maria also joined an after-school writing club where students are encouraged to write in any language they want, in any genre, and in any style. Freed from the constraints of formulaic writing that often characterizes their writing in English language arts (ELA) class, students in the writing club write stream of consciousness, free verse poetry, hip-hop lyrics, personal anecdotes, and short stories. In their pieces, complex voices become apparent. Maria, who struggles with writing in ELA class, where she follows simple formats and uses generic English expressions, is thriving in this setting. She chooses to write free verse poetry in both English and Spanish, translanguaging in writing like she does in everyday speech. She writes most adeptly in English, and so she composes most of her pieces in English. Yet, when she wants to convey a particular meaning, she reverts to Spanish to capture the distinction, as in her poem about her neighborhood:

> I am from the bright sun in the early mornings
> To the loud explosions from fireworks.
> From the bells of the *paleteros*
> ringing in the afternoons, urging kids to buy the *paletas*
> to the sizzling meat on the grill.
> I'm from the red clay river under the bridge where nothing goes
> to the spice of candy made from *tamarindos*
> From having social anxiety
> to the savory taste of *chicharones*
> I'm from the sizzling paper igniting fire
> to the sweet drink of *ochettas*
> I am from nature where I'm free and wild,
> to society where I'm small and quiet.

A week after Maria wrote the poem, Ms. Jordan, her ELA teacher, asks students to share their writing. At first, Maria hesitates; can she submit a poem partially in Spanish for her ELA class? She decides that she doesn't know how to translate those words into English while still capturing the essence of her neighborhood, so she decides to share her poem as is. The class listens attentively and then hands shoot up. Arthur asks what *paletas* are and where he could try some, and Beth wonders how candy can be spicy. Oscar comments about the tone of the piece, how it is sad and happy at the same time. Everyone seems to have something to say, and Maria seems a bit taller as she walks back to her seat.

Later, while reflecting on the day, Ms. Jordan comments privately that Maria's poem was a bit of a revelation; the girl who was always quiet and timid in class showed herself to have rich stories and languages with which to describe and engage with her life.

Richer Expression Options. When writing the poem above about her neighborhood, Maria was able to utilize language features of both her languages not only to better express her ideas but to also more richly and eloquently capture meanings. She used Spanish to not only showcase her bilingualism, but also her biculturalism and dual consciousness. By translanguaging, she authentically described the flavors of her neighborhood. By translanguaging in their writing and speaking, emergent bilinguals learn to label their world using the particular diction that carries certain meanings. They can describe the world with their intended meaning to bring forth a certain attitude toward a topic. In other words, translanguaging is about more than juggling languages to best meet one's intended meaning; translanguaging is about juggling one's perspective of the world. In a sense, translanguaging is also a type of transculturation where participants move across and between cultures as they attach meaning to words and phrases.

Embracing a Bilingual, Bicultural Identity. When translanguaging is done publicly as an activity that is not only condoned but also encouraged by the school, emergent and experienced bilinguals are able to share their multilingual selves with their peers and teachers and construct a positive and secure social identity that is bilingual and bicultural. Through sharing the above poem in her ELA class, Maria's classmates learned about her home life through forms of the language from which it was constructed. Some things about her neighborhood had been expressed in English, but for her to write about the place only in English would have been like describing a place that did not really exist. Her classmates learned not only a lot about Mexican culture, from its cuisine to its traditions, but also a lot about Maria. They saw Maria not only as another Mexican American girl, but as a unique individual who saw and experienced the world uniquely.

Socially, her participation in the writing club, and the connections she was able to make into her regular mainstream classrooms, proved to be a pivotal point for Maria. Her peers at school understood her more after hearing her bilingual translanguaging poems and encouraged her to write more; first the poem about her neighborhood and later on another poem about her mother's scary and exhausting trip across the border pregnant with her. Through these opportunities for sharing, her classmates were able to develop a better sense of where Maria came from and understood why she often teared up when she spoke about her mother. On her end, after reading these personal pieces with the full breadth of her voice, and seeing her peers' reactions, Maria felt more self-assured of her position in the classroom, in the school, and in her country. She felt her peers now welcomed her perspective and stories because they now empathized with her voice.

Also, it seemed that, as her peers learned more about her culture, they felt closer to her. Maria was often included in group projects in class, and her voice was honored more in the classroom and outside of class. Several of her classmates began inviting her to the movies and get-togethers at their houses, and Maria reported feeling more comfortable with her mainstream peers. Translanguaging connected all students linguistically and culturally and allowed them to see beyond her ethnicity or culture to an individual, a peer.

Majid: Bridging Meaning and Traditions

Majid came to Los Angeles 2 years ago from Pakistan as a 2nd-grader. His first language is Urdu, but he had begun studying English and French in primary school in his home country. Now, at age 9, he is entering 4th grade with Mrs. Roberts. At first, he did not know much academic English, but he was encouraged to write assignments in Urdu just to get him to record his thinking (at this point, his teacher only marked that he had done the work), while at the same time working to show how his English was developing. An ESL teacher came to his class, and sat by him to explain what the teacher was saying and to help him with his work. The ESL teacher and his homeroom teacher worked together closely to support his learning and his development as a bilingual person. They sought out resources in Urdu, they planned lessons with special adaptations to facilitate his learning, and they encouraged him to use all his languages to do his work.

Since Majid's English has become stronger, the ESL teacher is not as frequent a presence in his class, though Majid knows that she and Mrs. Roberts still work together a lot. He asks questions using the English words he knows, along with gestures and facial expressions. His classmates try to help him as well, encouraging Majid's contributions to the classroom. Majid often begins his comments with, "In Pakistan . . ." and talks about how things are similar or different, or presents stories and knowledge from his experience. His classmates have learned to construct meaning together with him, and seem to value his contributions because he often has something to offer that expands their knowledge and understandings.

Even though he is the only Pakistani student in his grade, he seems to be well integrated in the school as he is always with other classmates, many of whom are first-generation Asian Americans or Hispanic Americans. Since he can complete his work in Urdu, his writing and test responses are not constrained by his limited English ability. Though communication is still challenging at times and he does not understand everything that his teacher and classmates are saying, Majid feels a sense of accomplishment in the class, seeing that he is doing the same work as everyone else and that he is a part of the classroom culture.

The 4th-grade teacher, Mrs. Roberts, makes sure the tables where students are regularly seated include different language-speakers. She pairs EBs with native English speakers, EBs with native speakers and other EBs, and EBs from the same language backgrounds but with varying language needs. This way, classmates can support one another as needed. Majid is at a table with Chen Chen, a newcomer girl from China, and Sarah, who was born and grew up in Los Angeles. Majid and Sarah help Chen Chen in English reading and writing, but have found that they need help from her in math. Because her mom is a biologist, Sarah knows a lot about science, and Majid's dad has taught him a lot about computers. Each group member has a different expertise to share with the others.

In social studies the class is learning about different cultural traditions, specifically how people celebrate all over the world. The class first discusses U.S. celebration customs, such as sharing a meal and exchanging gifts. For the unit's class project, all of the students share their own family's cultural customs, as described below.

To share with the class, Noah brings his mother's famous matzo ball soup that they eat at Passover; Chen Chen brings some red firecrackers her family lights during Chinese New Year, and Kleber wears a traditional Carnival costume from Brazil. Sarah shows a video clip of her family celebrating UCLA's basketball championship by participating in the victory parade.

Majid, for his part, decides to show off a traditional Pakistani dance, the *bhangra*. He explains how his family and all the guests danced the *bhangra* at his sister's wedding last year, and that everyone had a great time. He first learned it by watching others do the dance, and then by practicing the dance in his room. Now he considers himself an expert. For his presentation he brings music from home, and wears a traditional costume his family gave him for his birthday.

As the music starts playing, the up-tempo beat fills the room. Majid jumps out to the front of the room from the hallway where he had put on his costume. The other students break into loud applause as they see him dressed in a red robe with a frilly red hat. As the music gets louder and the rhythm picks up, he starts his dance moves. He first lifts one leg, and then the other. He swings one arm over his head, and then the other. He dances back and forth, his body pulsating with the melody of the harmonium.

His classmates all cheer wildly as Majid enthusiastically swings his hips and twirls his arms. They have heard his writing filled with Urdu words about dancing the *bhangra*, and they are thrilled to finally be able to see it performed live. When he is done, everyone claps and clamors.

Through meaningful, welcoming experiences such as this, Majid not only gains confidence in his heritage, but also feels like he belongs in his school community. He is proud of his culture and the language of his traditions.

He is hopeful of his future here, where he can showcase the multiple dimensions of himself through ample and consistent affirming opportunities. Dancing the *bhangra* at school was significant not because it represented a rare opportunity for such sharing, but precisely because it was a natural part of an empowering translanguaging culture. In other words, what is notable here is that the cultural customs study in Majid's class was not a once-off cultural fair inserted in an otherwise monolingually and monoculturally oriented curriculum, but a unit that was one of many purposeful invitations for sharing and learning in a permeable, pluralistic environment. When he was dancing the *bhangra*, Majid was connected to his cultural past, to the thick history of Pakistan and the Asian subcontinent. As he danced, he relived the memories of family and cultural celebrations, of friends and acquaintances back home. Now, with his classmates so enthusiastic about the dance, he feels immersed in the culture of Pakistan and Los Angeles simultaneously.

Cassandra: Translanguaging Identity

Cassandra is settling into her 5th-grade class at her elementary school in a coastal city in Florida, having arrived in the United States 8 months before from Haiti. She had been moving from house to house after hurricanes devastated her home in Port-au-Prince.

In language arts class, her teacher, Mr. Klein, encourages her to express herself using whatever language she wants. She often writes in French, Haitian Creole, and English, intermixing and translanguaging among all three expressive varieties. Many of her classmates speak languages other than English as well. For the lesson today, Mr. Klein asks the students to write a personal narrative with vivid details. He gives students 20 minutes to draft.

> Because she can write about a story of her choice, Cassandra decides to go with a personal favorite: a story from her escapades with her best friend, Jameson, back in Haiti. For this assignment, she writes partially in Creole about the time she and Jameson went to Carnival celebrations downtown together. She describes the attire of people in the parade, the constant music, and wild dancing. They saw people in Carnival masks and people shouting wildly. The chaos was organized and choreographed, unlike the free-for-all of U.S. Mardi Gras traditions.
>
> In her writing, Cassandra tries to write most things in English so her classmates and teachers can understand, but descriptions of the music, costumes, and the expressions of the celebrations she writes in Haitian Creole. She describes the parade-goers shouting expressions like *lage ko'w!* (meaning "let go of yourself!") and *mete menn' anlè!* (meaning "put your hands in the air!"). Cassandra feels that this is more appropriate and faithful to the actual event, because she can preserve the ambiance and feel of those happy days. When she doesn't know how to describe

a Haitian memory in English, she uses her French or Haitian Creole. She knows that she and her teachers can use resources to translate her work as needed later on.

In fact, in Haiti she had not used only one language, but all three in conjunction. She learned to speak Haitian Creole growing up with her family members, and as she got into school, she began studying French and English. To only be able to write in English in her U.S. school would have limited the ways she expressed her being, those multilingual memories of her childhood. Even after just 8 months, Cassandra's grasp of the English language and of U.S. culture and customs is gaining steam. She has learned to chat with her friends, many of whom are dominant-culture classmates, using English. Slowly they also pick up some words from her other languages and begin using them in their group interactions. Instead of hampering her English acquisition, Cassandra's plurilingualism is an asset and social capital. She has gained more U.S. cultural and linguistic knowledge, while also nurturing pride in her Haitian language and heritage. She feels she is not letting go of Haiti in the United States, but holding each location with both hands, as shown in the following experience.

At one point in math, the class is learning about measurements and about the different units used to measure length. Cassandra immediately thinks of the bronze-colored Ishango bone that had been passed down in her family and become an heirloom. Her grandmother has told her that the bone had come from West Africa and was used as a tally stick. Cassandra often imagined it had magical powers, and secretly used it as a wand. She mentions this to Mr. Klein who asks if she would be willing to talk about it in class the next day. "What a great opportunity for your classmates to learn how people from different cultures thought about and measured things!" he says. Cassandra is so excited that her parents even allow her to bring the Ishango bone to school. Her classmates are fascinated and ask if they can hold it. Cassandra is hesitant about letting so many other people grab it, so she gives it to Mr. Klein to hold. One by one, the students come up to gently rub it, and gasp when they feel the ancient grooves on the bone.

To Cassandra, learning English in a translanguaging classroom does not create a competition between her heritage languages and the dominant language of her adoptive homeland, nor does it endanger her identity as a person of Haitian roots. Translanguaging is about a conjoining of her past memories in her heritage nation with her current experiences in the U.S. context. Classmates ask Cassandra how to say certain words in Haitian Creole, and they teach her how to say certain English words. Together they engage in a mutual negotiation of language, of translation of meaning, and transaction of ideas. In her mind, no one language is more powerful than another.

Making friends in Florida is different than in Haiti because of the language and cultural differences. She does not know many of the television shows or music they talk about. But Cassandra is also learning that deep down her U.S. friends here are not so different from her Haitian friends. They all dream of growing up and finding their way, and have similar worries, like what they would get for their next birthday or if their parents would punish them for fighting with their siblings. The linguistic barrier between English and her Haitian Creole seems arbitrary now that she has found so many commonalities with her peers. After visiting her friends' houses, she found that all parents scold their children when they misbehave, and all families laugh together the same as well. Their capacity to love even goes beyond their families. Since her family had lost almost everything in the hurricane, some of her classmates and parents donated some clothes and furniture to help them get settled into their new lives. The cultural barriers in her mind are slowly dissolving just as the language barriers in her academics are also being lifted.

Translanguaging pedagogy can have benefits for the adjustment of all students with diverse language backgrounds to learn in the same environment. When students' languages are not silenced, those languages can form social bonds and help construct a social identity for the students. Instead of being labeled "English-deficient," EB students are seen as "other-language-abled." Students move from a deficit identity to a multitalented identity. Their linguistic capital is enriched, and they feel more empowered to explore their social context, a context that welcomes and honors their multiple linguistic and cultural identities.

CONCLUSION

Friendships are very important for young people, for their mood, their social development, and their self-esteem. For EBs, friendships are trickier than for their mainstream counterparts, as they lack the linguistic and social knowledge related to majority culture that their mainstream peers take for granted. This can hamper their potential to successfully navigate these critical years. However, in translanguaging environments, Maria, Majid, and Cassandra were able to straddle both languages and cultures as they interacted with their social context. They maintained their previous identities while sculpting their new ones. In the process, they also learned more about their new worlds, while introducing their prior worlds to others. By doing so, they also broke the artificial constraints that led Chien to linguistic and social isolation and Emmanuel to a painful split between his public and his home identities. Through sharing translanguaging acts, classmates learn to see EBs differently: as individuals with rich stories, ideas, and knowledge, who are bilinguals in the making.

When EB students are branded as remedial or deficient, they are seen as lesser in the eyes of teachers, administrators, and peers. When English proficiency is the only measure of one's academic capability or worth, and their multilingualism is viewed as a hindrance to their English-speaking ability, they are given less social capital and are ostracized from the contexts of mainstream culture schools.

However, in schools and classrooms practicing and encouraging translanguaging, as both a pedagogical model and a philosophical outlook, the boundaries separating languages from each other and separating EBs from mainstream classmates become less pronounced. The social roles of English proficient classmates and teachers shift so that instead of being the ones who already have sufficient linguistic expertise, they also become students of other languages. In this context, individuals are both students and teachers, as they learn to see that these roles are not set in stone. Learning is not itemized in terms of language type, but becomes holistic and universal, able to extend into other parts of the students' lives. Social, geopolitical, and linguistic boundaries become understood as human constructs that students can overcome in the classroom. When they learn to communicate with one another using the full linguistic and cultural resources of the classroom, they develop multiple outlooks and a more global identity.

The social identities and relationships of all students, whether they be a native English speaker or an EL/EB, are very important for their growth and development into adults. In a translanguaging setting emergent and experienced bilingual students can be repositioned as powerful cultural and linguistic resources. They can also develop greater self-esteem and confidence, which in turn facilitates their own English language and U.S. culture acquisition. They can become full-fledged members of the learning community and of mainstream society.

CHAPTER 4

Meeting School Challenges

As we noted in Chapter 1, emergent bilingual students are a fast-growing population in American schools. According to the Institute of Education Sciences, in 2014–2015 there were 4.8 million public school students who received ESL services, making up 9.5% of the total student population. This was 300,000 students more than the equivalent number for 2004–2005 (NCES, 2017). According to the same document, during this period all but 15 states saw an increase in their EL student population.

With the increase in immigrant students and students identified as English learners (over 50% of whom are U.S.-born) across the country, public schools are facing tremendous pressures to get these students up to their grade-level benchmarks as required by the Common Core State Standards and the Every Student Succeeds Act (ESSA), and to graduate on time with their peers. However, there is a great shortage of certified ESL and bilingual teachers in almost every state with increasing numbers of new immigrants and emergent bilinguals.

In reviewing the Reaching English Learners Act, Corey Mitchell (2018) stated that "the U.S. Department of Education reported that at least 32 states have a shortage of teachers to work with English-learners, but the problem is not new. School districts have struggled for decades to find qualified bilingual teachers, especially in communities where English is not the first language for many students" (p. 1). According to the survey results of the McGraw-Hill EL Education (2017) Report:

- Only 39% of the teachers and administrators surveyed strongly agreed with the statement "I have received enough EL training/professional development" (p. 21), and 82% of respondents reported spending personal time and effort to develop their skills to support English learners.
- "Newer EL educators (those who have worked in EL education for less than 2 years) are significantly less confident than more experienced educators in their EL training and development," with only 36 percent of new respondents feeling "they have received enough professional development compared to 70 percent of more experienced educators" (p. 4).

In this chapter we present, with interview and observation data, the challenges schools encounter in educating emergent bilinguals with diverse language backgrounds in both bilingual and ESL programs. The chapter also includes examples of schools and classrooms using a translanguaging model to meet their students' needs and navigate the challenges of teacher shortages and limited budgets and school resources.

BILINGUAL EDUCATION: CHALLENGES AND SOLUTIONS

Bilingual programs in U.S. schools are mostly transitional programs, where students identified as English learners usually study the content subjects in their first language while developing their English language skills. In a bit of a misnomer, these home language classes are often referred to as *bilingual classes* to differentiate them from language arts and content classes taught in English. But with EBs of many different home languages, it is impossible for any school to provide bilingual education to meet the needs of all their emergent bilinguals in this way.

Shortages of Financial Resources and Qualified Teachers

Budget is an issue. In New York City school districts, for instance, if there are not enough EBs with the same home language background to make a class of 30 at the middle school level, a school is not allowed to hire a teacher for a bilingual class. Once we saw 43 students in a bilingual class in a New York City school, and were told the school was waiting to have enough newcomers to make a second class, at which point they could hire an extra teacher. Sometimes, the school had to wait until spring to have enough newcomers to make another class. Before then, newcomers, with different home language backgrounds, were just put into existing classes, which could become quite crowded and hamper teaching and learning.

One day in a middle school in New York City, Danling saw a Black girl in a Chinese bilingual class, so she asked the principal why this student was in this class. Here was his response:

> I have a range of students, from arriving here only a week ago to a year or two, speaking 23 different languages in my school. I can barely find enough licensed ESL teachers, let alone qualified bilingual teachers. I only have Chinese and Spanish bilingual programs in my school, as we have a large number of Chinese- and Spanish-speaking students to make the programs. But with other [EB] students, that is what I can do: either let them stay in the mainstream classes (with some ESL services) or I put all Asian students, such as Vietnamese, Cambodians, Tibetans, Philippinos, Malaysians, Japanese, Koreans, or Thais, into the Chinese

bilingual classrooms. Sometimes, I even put some Africans into the Chinese bilingual classes. And the others, I just put them in the Spanish bilingual program.

Subsequently, Danling (D) interviewed a female student from Kenya (S) in the Chinese bilingual class:

D: How did you get to this program?
S: I don't know. They just put me here.
D: You don't live in the neighborhood; why do you come to this school?
S: My mom said this school is better; no gangs, better students and teachers, so she put me here.
D: How do you get here every day?
S: Subway, then bus; it takes me over an hour each way.
D: Do you like to be in this class?
S: It is okay. The students and teacher are nice to me. Sometimes, they give me their Chinese food and snacks. I love them, delicious.
D: Have you learned any Chinese?
S: Some words, like *nihao* (hello), *xie-xie* (thank you), *zaijian* (goodbye).
D: Did you learn anything else in this class?
S: Not much. Sometimes, the teacher would let me read the English books and let me do my other work here.

As the principal stated above, since there were not enough students with a common first language other than Chinese and Spanish in his school, he had no way to provide home language bilingual education for non-Chinese-speaking or non-Spanish-speaking students. Traditionally, most new immigrants choose to stay in neighborhoods with their ethnic community, and children with the same ethnic background tend to go to the same neighborhood schools. However, as the principal noted and as national language data suggest (U.S. Census Bureau, 2015), even in schools with high concentrations of specific ethnic backgrounds, the student population can still be very diverse. For instance, in New York Chinatown schools with majority Chinese students, there are some students of Hispanic backgrounds as well as some from other Asian countries. Students either reside within the school zone or, as in the case of the student interviewed above, choose their schools for quality and safety reasons. It is distressing to see those students venturing so far to go to school, yet still not receiving the quality of education their families expect.

In schools with transitional bilingual programs, the idea is for students to receive content-area instruction in their home languages until their English is strong enough for them to progressively transition to English-only instruction. When the school fails to provide bilingual education for students whose home languages do not have enough speakers in the school to warrant a special section, those students are often put in regular classes to be dragged along with their English-proficient peers. Otherwise, they may be placed in any available bilingual program to study in an unfamiliar language with peers who grew up around that language. In both situations, those students are basically marking time in schools, and their teachers don't know what to do with them, or what or how to teach them.

A shortage of highly qualified bilingual teachers is another issue. Ideally, bilingual teachers should fluently speak and be literate in both languages, be knowledgeable in a subject area, and also be prepared in bilingual and ESL instructional methodology. However, it is not easy to find bilingual teachers to meet all these requirements, especially at the secondary level. Through our work in schools over the past 2 decades, we have found that most bilingual teachers fall within the following categories:

- Fluent speakers of two languages (home language and English), literate in both languages, but without any specialized content knowledge, and with little to no training in bilingual or ESL education
- Fluent speakers of two languages, literate in only one language, without any specialized content knowledge, and with some preparation in bilingual or ESL education
- Speakers of their home language and literate in it, but with minimal knowledge of English; specialized in one content knowledge (math, science, or social studies); and with little to no bilingual or ESL education training

Because of the shortage of bilingual teachers, often people only need to pass simple written tests in two languages (English and another language) to get a temporary teaching certificate; then they start teaching a bilingual class without any practicum experience either in content or in bilingual or ESL instruction. These teachers have to teach bilingual students through trial and error, and many end up leaving teaching forever after a few years.

Because it is hard to find qualified bilingual teachers in the United States, schools often go abroad to find them. In a middle school in New York's Spanish Harlem, we found that all the math and science bilingual teachers were hired directly from Mexico or other Spanish-speaking countries. Often, the teachers could barely speak or understand any English. In addition, having experienced different teacher preparation and schooling contexts in their home countries, they struggled with understanding and using norms and practices, both cultural and pedagogic, common in U.S. schools. Many were unfamiliar with scaffolding instruction, organizing and conducting group activities, and teaching reading/writing in the content areas. Classroom management also became a significant challenge, as their cultural expectations for classroom routines and appropriate student behavior clashed with those of the students.

We also found the same case in an elementary school in the Atlanta area, where through international headhunters, a few teachers from China were hired for the school's English-Chinese dual language immersion program. Though on the surface a reasonable idea, the reality of the initiative revealed significant shortcomings. The Chinese teachers spoke little English, had never taught elementary-aged children, and were only accustomed to teaching through lecture and used a traditional, text-bound approach. When they started teaching elementary children in a U.S. school, they were totally lost and couldn't keep the children engaged and well-behaved. They were shocked that they had to be with the children all day long and had to teach multiple subjects, as is common practice for elementary school teachers in the United States.

Since bilingual education started nearly half a century ago in the United States, budget issues and the shortage of qualified bilingual teachers have always been critical issues in providing adequate bilingual education for all emergent bilinguals. This is one of the major reasons why bilingual education has been ineffective at educating emergent bilingual students in many school districts, and why bilingual education was abandoned in many parts of the United States. Such inadequate implementations of bilingual education have given rise to doubts expressed by the public and to questions from policymakers as to whether bilingual education is in fact the best way to help emergent bilinguals keep pace with their English-proficient peers in terms of their school learning.

A Multilingual K–5 School

In the preceding section, we discussed how budgetary constraints and shortages of highly qualified bilingual teachers present significant challenges to teachers and institutions as they work to support the learning of their emergent bilingual students. In what follows, we present stories of how a translanguaging model can be adopted to meet these challenges.

> In this K–5 school in New York City, the students speak 26 different languages at home. When you walk into the school, you can see "Welcome" written in 26 languages at the entrance of the front office. On the adjacent wall, there is a list of names of the students and the languages they speak. When a new student arrives, a current student who speaks the newcomer's language will be called to act as a guide: escorting the new student to class, giving this student an orientation of the school, and introducing this student to the teacher and fellow classmates. The guide would serve as host for a week until the newcomer gets familiar with the school schedule and community. This happens year-round, and the students at the school play central roles in welcoming new students and orienting them to their new environment. This practice has become a valued custom in the school, and

students are proud to take on the responsibility and love to be called upon to host newcomers.

In the front office, information about the students' parents and guardians is on file. The records list their home countries and languages, occupations, professional and technical skills, hobbies, and interests, including their available time to volunteer at the school as well as their contact information. The parents or guardians are often invited to give guest lectures, demonstrate lessons, or help with class projects. As the teachers at this school have said, "We can always find experts among our students' family members for just about everything and on any topics." The family members don't have to speak English when they give talks to any class, as their children or other children in the class can act as translators. Children clamor to have their parents or family members come to the school to visit or give talks, and they love to translate for their parents or other speakers of their heritage tongue. The parents and relatives feel comfortable in their children's school. They make their best effort to contribute their expertise to the school when they are called upon to help.

Students as School Resources. This school sees their students' diverse language backgrounds as a resource. Letting children be the guides for new students, especially those who are new to the country and to the U.S. school system, is the best way to orient newcomers to a novel environment. It not only reduces the burden for the school and classroom teachers, but it also makes the host-students feel that they are important members of the school community, giving them a sense of responsibility, agency, and pride. This practice also explicitly positions students as skilled language and cultural brokers whose bilingualism and bicultural knowledge is a valuable asset that can help others in unique and important ways. In addition, the new students feel less overwhelmed by the novelty of everything and have a smoother transition as their peer guides help them figure out rules, schedules, and routines so they can keep up with their class, and quickly become part of the school community. Moving to a new school can be daunting for any child, and this is even more challenging when the move is to a new country where everything seems foreign and strange. A peer who can speak the newcomer's language and act as a friend provides critical support.

Schools who serve vibrant immigrant communities, such as those in New York City, tend to have new students arrive year-round, some even during the last month of school, and most of these latecomers are new immigrant students. Helping students become oriented to a new environment can be time-consuming. The practice of peer guides preserves school resources, as the school doesn't have to take as much time from an ESL teacher or a staff member or aide to help new students acclimate to the school. In addition, it provides substantial support to classroom teachers who work to facilitate student access to ongoing learning in the classroom. With the support of a peer who can explain classroom routines and procedures, teachers can better concentrate on the students' academic learning. Indeed, it can be argued that none of the adults in school can do what peers can do for newcomers, as they can use their shared language, generational know-how, personal experiences, and learning skills to help their new classmates orient to the school environment and the class community.

Students' Families as School Resources. Students' parents and other family members are great resources for schools, especially those of diverse cultural and linguistic backgrounds. They can share valuable knowledge and experiences students can't learn from reading or from their own lived experience. When parents and family members realize that the school values their knowledge, expertise, culture, and language, they will feel more a part of their children's school learning and develop rapport with school personnel. This leads to children feeling proud of their parents and the unique knowledge they have, instead of feeling ashamed of them because they can't speak English well or because they look or behave differently. When the children translate for their parents during presentations, they demonstrate their bilingual competence, biliterate ability, and their knowledge of their home culture and country. They also get to experience firsthand the roles bilinguals can play in facilitating communication and intercultural understanding, and practice their skills as translators and cultural brokers. What a great way to celebrate different cultures, languages, and world experiences and educate all children to expand their knowledge and worldviews to become global citizens! Our students and their families are valuable resources for our bilingual education. They are dependable resources a school can rely on not only to meet the challenges of teacher shortage, but also to provide rich education and build a connected community for all students.

A Bilingual Social Studies Class

In this section we provide an example of a bilingual class in which the teacher used translanguaging to integrate social studies content and drew on EB's family members to contribute to class learning.

This class is in a transitional bilingual program in a middle school in New York's Chinatown, where Chinese is supposed to be the language of instruction, with a majority of the students being Chinese. Mr. Wang, the classroom teacher, is a native speaker of Chinese and is literate in English. When the school decided to integrate social studies content into this bilingual class, the first challenge for teachers was finding books written in Chinese on the social studies topics in the grade curriculum. The social studies curriculum for the grade focused on U.S. history: from pre-Columbian Native American civilizations, to the Pilgrims, the American Revolution, the Civil

War, up to the Korean and Vietnam wars, and the current war on terror. The experiences of the students in this class vary widely, from being in the United States for over 2 years to having arrived just a month ago. Most students speak Chinese; a few are Spanish speakers, two came from the Middle East and speak a variety of Arabic dialects, one is from Vietnam, and another is from the Democratic Republic of the Congo and speaks Swahili and French. Mr. Wang has decided to include not only Chinese books as teaching materials, but also English picture books on the American history topics covered in class. In addition, he asks students to search in local libraries, on bookshelves at home, and online for reading materials in English or their home languages on these topics. These resources would be used as part of their reading in class and at home. As homework, the students are encouraged to watch online videos (via YouTube or other services) in English or their home languages on the American history topics they are studying.

In class, students are grouped in teams of five or six to discuss their reading. Mr. Wang joins the group of non-Chinese-speaking students. They read some English picture books and books they found in their home languages. The group shares the English picture books they read as a group. Mr. Wang encourages students to write in their reading journals in the language of their choice. The other groups have their discussion mostly in Chinese, even when talking about the books they read in English, conversations that mix in English vocabulary they learned from the English texts.

One of the final projects for the class is a group research project: Each group is asked to choose one American history topic from those addressed in social studies for deeper, more focused study. As a group, they are to study resources about their selected topic, discuss the information encountered in their research, and then create a poster about their topic to present to the class. The group resources—which could be print or online texts, videos, and community resources—can be in any language the students decide. In their discussion groups, they can also use any language, as long as they don't exclude any fellow group members. Drafts of writing can be composed in any language, but the final posters have to be bi- or multilingual: home language and English, so everyone can understand their work. The students delve into this project with gusto. They seek reading materials on the Internet, inside the school, and at local libraries. Some parents take their children to local museums and some students even find people in the community to interview who had been involved in the Korean and Vietnam wars. The Vietnamese-speaking student actually interviews her own family members about their experiences during the Vietnam War.

For the bilingual group poster, the students use Google Translate and other translation software to support their translation efforts, and Mr. Wang helps with the final editing. Each group presents their posters to the class; one group member reads the writing in their home language, and another reads in English. The group with the only Vietnamese student has their poster in three languages: Chinese, English, and Vietnamese. Another group has their poster in four languages: English, Spanish, Arabic, and Swahili. No students are left out in this project regardless of whether they are new arrivals, have a home language other than Chinese, or are the sole speakers of a particular language. The students show great interest in reading and listening to a language different from their own, and they have fun learning some relevant vocabulary in different languages.

During the last week of the class, two guest speakers are invited to the class to give talks: One is the uncle of the Vietnamese student who shares his own experience during the Vietnam War, and the other is the grandfather of a Chinese student and a Korean War veteran, who reminisces about his experience during that war. The visitors speak in their home languages, as the teacher and students help with the translations.

From the Vietnamese uncle, the students learn that to the Vietnamese, the Americans were invaders of their country, bombing their land, burning their houses, and killing their people. They call it the American War rather than the Vietnam War. From the Chinese grandfather, the students learn that thousands of Chinese soldiers were bombed and killed before they even had a chance to pick up their guns to fight, and that the 28-year-old son of Chairman Mao, the Communist Party leader, was among the dead.

The guest speakers' personal perspectives and experiences during the wars give the class a nuanced and complex understanding of those wars, seeing history through another point of view, that no reading alone could have accomplished. Through these two talks, Mr. Wang and his students gain tremendous knowledge about the two Asian wars in which the United States was involved, as well as respect for the speakers. This knowledge and empathy broaden their horizons and enrich their understandings and open their minds. Even the student-relatives of the two speakers comment that they had never before heard the stories their uncle and grandfather shared and that, prior to this, they knew very little about their war experiences.

Teaching and Learning with a Translanguaging Model. The bilingual teacher, Mr. Wang, in this class was a fluent bilingual speaker and biliterate in both Chinese and English. But he was not well versed in social studies and had very little education in ESOL and bilingual pedagogy. Mr. Wang had taught Chinese language arts (Chinese language, history, and literature) in the bilingual program for a few years and this was his 2nd year teaching the bilingual program integrated with the grade-level social studies curriculum. To be able to teach this new curriculum, Mr. Wang had to learn a new subject and consider ways of integrating bilingual language objectives with social studies objectives. He stated that his biggest challenges were identifying materials in Chinese that were well matched to the social studies learning objectives and figuring out how to work with the several non-Chinese students in his classroom. When he learned about the translanguaging model, which allowed students to read, write, and discuss in any languages (home language or English) that could maximize their learning potential, Mr. Wang felt relieved and liberated as this practice enabled him to include and engage all students from diverse backgrounds to work and move together through the curriculum.

Using Multilingual and Multimodal Texts. Usually, a transitional bilingual class is integrated with a subject area so that emergent bilingual students can study the grade-level curriculum in their native language while simultaneously developing their English proficiency. However, finding appropriate textbooks written in EBs' native languages on all the topics required by the grade-level curriculum is not an easy task. Indeed, in the case of the bilingual social studies class discussed above, finding an appropriate Chinese-language textbook for middle school and satisfactorily covering all the requisite U.S. history topics is all but impossible. This becomes exponentially more challenging when more than one native language is spoken among the students. A translanguaging model allows students to move beyond textbooks and read a variety of print or digital texts, including YouTube and other videos in any language, on the topics they are studying. In translanguaging classrooms, teachers create opportunities and spaces for students to discuss their reading, draft and revise their work in the languages of students' choice, and in the end, to produce bi/multilingual and often multimodal work to present to the class. Through translanguaging, the responsibility of identifying relevant and appropriate academic resources is no longer solely on the teacher's shoulders, but a task shared by the entire class community. Though teachers in translanguaging classrooms do identify and make available some resources to the students, they also focus on guiding students to look for and evaluate reading materials in various languages, work in small groups, search for resources, and write, translate, edit, publish, and present their work.

Developing Both Language and Content Knowledge. In a translanguaging bi- or multilingual classroom, students are able to simultaneously develop both their native and English language skills, along with the content knowledge. Through reading, discussing, and writing in their first languages, the students continue developing that language. Translating their native language into English helps students develop their English language skills, as well as their metalinguistic competence. A translanguaging model does not ignore or segregate any of the language resources of students, but uses any language students choose to accrue content knowledge. It is truly a multilingual paradigm that not only engages all of the students' languages in the service of content-area learning, but also supports students in learning how to be effective multilinguals.

Students in a translanguaging bilingual class can learn grade-level content knowledge while developing academic English, and they can gradually choose to read developmentally appropriate English texts. The students themselves are in control of their learning, as they are allowed to use any languages in their reading, discussion, and writing to ensure they learn the content knowledge most efficiently and effectively. In this class, they do not feel they are learning in remedial programs, as they are learning the same content knowledge at the same pace as their English-proficient peers.

Participating in an Inclusive Learning Community. In a bilingual classroom, students may not only have different native languages, but also varying proficiencies in those languages. Additionally, their English abilities as well as total schooling duration may be distinct. In the translanguaging bilingual classroom described above, we can see that every student's home language is included as part of the content learning: in-class activity, out-of-class work, and final assessment and presentations. The students who are able to read English can choose to read, speak, and write in English any time they want to. Often, these students would traverse between languages. For instance, when the topics become too difficult to read in English, they will switch back to reading in their heritage languages. These students also function as language experts, assisting other students with translating their works into English for their final presentations so other students in class can understand their work.

All languages in a translanguaging class share an equal status, with no hierarchy defining them, and all students are respected learners, engaging in vigorous learning, despite being either in the United States for several years, new arrivals, or the only person with a particular native language. They enjoy one another's language, background, and expertise with certain skills and knowledge. A translanguaging classroom is like a version of the United Nations, where all members try their best to contribute to the learning community.

In translanguaging bilingual classrooms, teachers do not see themselves as the experts in everything, but as co-learners along with their students in terms of both content and languages. They guide students in searching for reading materials and resources in their native languages and English, creating spaces, providing opportunities, and giving time for students to work together in and out of class to use their chosen languages individually or as a group to maximize their learning potentials. Families and community members are counted on as support and resources: They help students with their research on certain topics, take them to museums or bookstores, and come to the class to share their knowledge and personal experiences related to class topics. In this kind of classroom, you can see students reading, speaking, and writing in different languages and producing and publishing their multilingual work. Everyone is busy working and engaging in learning, and no one is sitting idle or neglected in this inclusive learning community.

ESL EDUCATION FOR EMERGENT BILINGUALS

To expand our discussion of the efficacy of the translanguaging model, we now shift attention from bilingual education to ESL education for emerging bilinguals. The challenges to effective ESL education are similar to those of bilingual education.

Challenges Faced by ESL Efforts

Most certified ESL teachers are specialists in applied linguistics with second language pedagogy. With the high demand of curriculum requirements and increasing numbers of emergent bilinguals in school districts across the country, there is a palpable shortage of certified ESL teachers, especially in the states traditionally having fewer immigrants. An ESL teacher from Alabama expresses her frustration over this situation:

> In our district we have about 200 students who need ESL services, and I am the only teacher in about 20 schools. I travel to different schools each day to work with those students. I see some students once a week, some once every other week or a month, and some I never get a chance to see at all. Even when I do see them, I have so much assessment and paperwork to do, I barely have time to teach anything. I don't know if I really am an ESL teacher, or just a staff member who occasionally checks on these students, making sure they are in school and receive enough attention.

This teacher's circumstance is not unusual in the United States. As Wilson Criscione (2018) reported recently about EL education in Idaho schools, "of schools with at least 20 English-learner students, about a quarter didn't have an English language development teacher at all in 2016–2017" (p. 1). The shortage of certified ESL teachers is a common issue in many school districts across the nation, including those metropolises that continue to see a high influx of new immigrants like New York City, Los Angeles, and Houston. Not only must many ESL teachers travel from classroom to classroom within a school, but in some districts, they often have to travel to different schools to serve emergent bilinguals who need ESL services.

As evident in the teacher's comments above, in addition to teaching students with different levels and needs, paperwork regarding assessment and compliance takes much of the ESL teachers' time. With high demands from state standards and arduous expectations for tracking and reporting the progress of students who need ESL services, emergent bilinguals are given an ever-increasing number of tests. One ESL teacher from New York City said that in the space of a single school year, she had to give nine different tests to her EBs, including individual tests for certain students, placement tests, and tests on different subjects or areas. In the end she lamented, "They have no time for study, but just take one test after another." Teachers have no time to teach; students have no time to learn. The time demands of these different kinds of assessments significantly cut into instructional time that ideally should be used for school learning. This is a common and valid concern for all students, but it is particularly problematic for emergent bilinguals who need more time and help to learn a new language and content knowledge to keep pace with their English-proficient peers.

In pull-out ESL programs EBs are taken out of their regular classroom and into resource rooms for language-focused instruction, as we portrayed in Chapter 2 with the story of Rosa. To avoid the instructional time loss that comes with this practice and to help EBs keep pace with their peers in the regular classroom, push-in ESL was created to provide service for EBs in regular classrooms. Though the idea sounds appealing, the practice has challenges. Below we hear a push-in ESL teacher's frustration:

> I am in charge of 23 ELs from grades 3–5, and they are spread across six different classrooms (two to five in one room). I try to see them every other day if I can, though I should see them every day. But it is hard when I have to work with them in different classrooms. The worst part is: I can't see them all during their reading or language arts time, so I may get in when they have math, science, or even PE and art. I am supposed to work with them based on the curriculum of their grade, and help them with whatever their mainstream class teachers are teaching. This makes my work very hard. How can I work with so many teachers in different grades, to know what they are teaching on different subject areas? Do I have any spare time? Or do the teachers have any spare time to talk to me? I am scurrying like a crazy rat, all over the building, barely having any time for a lunch break. I have so much paperwork regarding compliance, assessment, and communication with their parents and guardians. When I work with the students in their classrooms, I help them with their class assignments more than teaching them anything. I feel like I am treated like a paraprofessional, not like a licensed ESL professional. I have my own curriculum too, but I never get to teach it.

This is a complaint we have heard often from push-in ESL teachers. When ESL teachers get so frustrated and overwhelmed, as with the case above, it becomes impossible to teach students effectively. Many programs like ESL or different types of bilingual programs have been developed to give emergent bilingual students extra or special instructional support to keep pace with their learning. However, a shortage of teachers and severe budgetary constraints have made it impossible to serve emergent bilinguals fully, with sensitivity to their individual learning needs. As this teacher expressed, the overwhelming responsibilities and expectations placed upon

ESL teachers make them feel undervalued and disrespected, and undermine their professional identities. It is an excellent idea to have ESL and classroom teachers work together to help their shared students learn better, but with hectic school schedules, teachers don't have time to collaborate with their ESL colleagues, and they often have to use their prep time or lunch time or stay late after the school to help those students who need extra assistance.

Meanwhile, ESL teachers have to work with students in different grades encompassing a wide range of language resources and literacy backgrounds, previous school experience, and length of time in U.S. schools. No matter whether they are working in pull-out or push-in ESL programs, these teachers can be stretched very thin in serving all the ELs in their classrooms or caseloads. Therefore, these students may not get the help and support they need and their slow progress frustrates both classroom and ESL teachers, who often end up blaming each other. The following are excerpts from two separate meetings an ESL program director had with a high school English teacher and an ESL teacher who shared the same EL student.

> **The English Teacher:** I don't know why they put this student in my class. This placement is crazy, because he barely understands anything in my class, and I don't know what the ESL teacher has done with him. She is supposed to build his English basic skills so he can learn in my class. But he seems to understand nothing. This is 11th grade, and I used a 7th-grade vocabulary book, and he still can't do it. What I am supposed to do with him?

> **The ESL teacher:** She [the English teacher] can't use the high school textbook to teach him! This student was tested as level 1 in the English proficiency test and, since his English is so low, I had no way to use a common standard to assess his English ability but, if I had to take a guess, I would say he is only at a 3- to 4-year-old level at best. The classroom teachers have to adjust their teaching and expectations, not just use lower-grade textbooks to teach him or think of him as a high school student who is just a little behind. There is no way he can learn with books he barely understands anything out of. It is not fair for them to blame us. It takes time for these students to develop their language and content knowledge. They came to us knowing nothing about school.

Both of the teachers have valid perspectives. ESL education is intended to help EBs develop their English language ability so they can move to the regular classes to study along with their English-proficient peers. But as we explained in Chapter 2, it often takes 2–3 years for EBs to develop their communicative English and 3–5 years or more to develop their academic language in order to study along with their peers (Cummins, 1981a). Hakuta (2011) and Hopkins, Thompson, Linquanti, Hakuta, and August (2013) affirm that acquiring academic proficiency takes 7 years or longer, and they add that factors such as individual student characteristics and quality of services are also important. Indeed, students like the one discussed above, whose formal education was interrupted, require a much longer period of time before they are able to study alongside their English-proficient peers. But in our schools, teachers and students don't have the much-needed luxury of time. Instead, they are often working in overwhelming situations trying to achieve unrealistic or impossible goals.

An ESL Translanguaging Classroom

As we have demonstrated earlier, translanguaging pedagogy may provide some alternative ways to meet the challenges in teaching emergent bilinguals in current school situations. In this section, we share how the translanguaging model works in a pull-out ESL classroom. This is an ESL beginning class with 22 2nd- and 3rd-grade students: four from China, seven from Spanish-speaking countries, three from India, two from Vietnam, two from Thailand, two from Japan, one from Denmark, and one from Poland. They have been in the United States from a few weeks to a few months. The ESL teacher, Ms. Huang, speaks English and Cantonese, knows a few Spanish words, but can only read and write in English. In the lesson below, she focuses on food names.

Following a general discussion of food based upon a shared reading of a big book on different food names, Ms. Huang writes, "I like hamburgers," on the board and also draws a picture of a hamburger by the sentence. She invites her students to come to the board to write and draw what they like to eat from their own cultures and in their languages. The students from different language groups walk to the front, and add their words to the beginning stem "I like . . ." and also draw a picture of their favorite food. Here are a few samples from each language:

I like *jiaozi.* (Chinese)
I like *pierogi.* (Polish)
I like *satay gain.* (Thai)
I like *yakitori* chicken. (Japanese)
I like *samosas.* (Hindi)
I like *empanadas.* (Spanish)
I like *frikadeller.* (Danish)

The students can write either in their home language or in English letter–sound spelling. The rest of the class watches and helps with the English spelling when a student cannot figure out the letters from just listening to the sounds of the words that the teacher pronounces. The students who do not know the words guess the meaning based on the drawings accompanying the words. The students are not only learning new words, but also new varieties of food from different cultures. After the students from each language group had a turn sharing their favorite food on the board, Ms. Huang turns to the class and says:

> Great! We are learning so many new foods and words in different languages and cultures, many I had never heard of myself. Now I know how to order when I go to different restaurants. We can make a class book called "What We Like to Eat Together." For your homework today, I'd like you to make your own book of "What My Family and I Like to Eat." You can draft the writing in any language, and we can translate your work into English later, so we can learn English and also about the food in our home countries. If you want, you can add more ideas into your writing. For instance: When do you usually eat this food? For breakfast, lunch, or dinner? Every day or only on a special holiday? Who is the best cook in your house?

In this lesson, the ESL teacher not only taught students how to express themselves with words and pictures and learn about one another's languages and cultures, but she also reviewed letter–sound associations in English, a concept they had been working on. With the help of their family members, the students each made a bilingual picture book of the food their family loved to eat. They shared their books with the class, and the whole class learned a lot about foods in different cultures, and had a lot of fun learning how to say the names of foods their peers introduced. They also created a class book titled *The Food We Love to Eat* with each student contributing a page. Each page of the class book includes English with another language, and features a special food from a country or a region of a country.

To differentiate her instruction, Ms. Huang encourages the students who are more proficient in English to use the vocabulary and sentence structures they have learned to add more content and details to their writing. All the student-written books are in the class library, and students can read one another's work during reading workshop time or they can borrow the books to read at home. Ms. Huang reported that her students love to read the books written by them or their peers, and are proud of their own words and pictures. She spoke further about the value of this class library:

> Beyond being a valuable learning activity for the authors, bilingual student–written books can be wonderful as reading materials for their peers and for future students. Having these books in my classroom library really helps with the challenge of finding appropriate books for my students. I often have students with seven or eight different native languages in my class, with a wide range of different English and first language literacy abilities. It is so hard to find the right books for this diverse population. I start with family, school, and community vocabulary, and later on we move more into the content areas. It is almost impossible to find bilingual books with these topics written in different

languages. So we create our books together, with the help of dictionary, translation software, and oral translation programs, as well as students' family members. We write and we read, and we learn English and each other's languages together.

Given that the stated objective of traditional ESL education is the acquisition of English language proficiency, most ESL classes adopt an English-only policy. Ms. Huang used to do the same. She believed that English-only was the way to maximize students' English learning opportunities and to push them to develop English skills efficiently. With a wide range of native languages and English abilities, she had a very hard time working with her students as a group. However, she also had no time to work with students one-on-one, so she felt that many students were left unattended. She would see them walking back and forth between her room and their regular class and thought that they were just marking time; week after week, those students made little to no progress.

As she was learning about translanguaging, Ms. Huang began to question the wisdom of English-only approaches that, up until then, she had considered self-evident. As she transitioned to a translanguaging model, Ms. Huang began to invite students' home languages into her classroom. She encouraged students with the same home language to work together in their native language to discuss the English language or subject concepts she was teaching. She also let students with stronger English abilities explain what she taught to other students in their shared home language. In this way her understanding of her role as an ESL teacher shifted. In the past, she had wished for more time to work individually with each student because she believed that she was the only one who could support their English progress, that only she could reach every student. Now she understands that there is so much learning accomplished by students working together. So she lets students help one another, reteach what she has already taught, and discuss the learning together. When students are empowered to assist and teach one another, they think more deeply about the content and are proud to be acknowledged not just as learners but also as knowers. "This also frees me to work with the students who have no one in the class who shares their home language, or to do more targeted work with individual students or small groups," Ms. Huang added. Trying a new model has many challenges, as Ms. Huang expressed:

It feels good to see students so engaged and involved in their learning. But sometimes I also am nervous, wondering if I let them use their native language in my room too much. My job is to help them develop their English skills as soon as possible, so they can pass the English language tests and be mainstreamed. But I have to say that most students do want to learn English and use it as much as they can; they don't just hide behind their home languages. I'm probably the one who doesn't know how to find a balance. I am learning and taking the risk.

Yes, trying a new model is taking a risk. Sometimes it requires us to transform our views of teaching and learning, reorganize our teaching space, and readjust our relationship with our students. And often, as pioneers, we have to struggle against oppositional forces to incite real change.

TRANSLANGUAGING PRACTICE IN A MAINSTREAM CLASSROOM

In the final example of this chapter, we show another teacher taking on the challenge of using the translanguaging model. This time we visit a mainstream classroom in which the teacher worked to include all students and their different language backgrounds in his instruction and maximize their learning potential.

The teacher in this 5th-grade class, Mr. Miller is a native English speaker who learned Spanish as a foreign language. In this class, besides monolingual English-speaking students, there are students who speak Spanish, Polish, Arabic, and Russian. On the whiteboard in the front of the classroom, learning objectives, the class schedule, and homework assignments are written in five different languages. The word wall at the back of the room also features all five languages. When we asked Mr. Miller if he did all the translation, he said:

> I guess, I have known for a while that it is important to involve students' languages in the classroom, so I used to take it upon myself to translate words, objectives, and essential questions. I often asked the parents and friends for help or used translation software. Then, I realized that beyond the fact that this was a very time-consuming process, I was taking a valuable learning opportunity away from the students. Now I let the students do it. They use the help of their parents and family members and they love it! This can get them engaged in learning and even let their parents know what unit or lesson we are working on. Just like I want them to own their new vocabulary, I want them to own the class, to make it theirs. All students feel part of the community and are affirmed as experts in some way with translanguaging practice.

In this mainstream class among the majority of monolingual English speakers, there are advanced bilingual students who have passed their English proficiency tests and are no longer receiving ESL services, as well as emergent bilinguals at various levels of English language proficiency who need ESL service daily or two to three times a week. All of these bilingual students, advanced and emergent, need some support to have full access to lessons and to keep pace with their native English-speaking peers. In addition, they need opportunities to use all their linguistic resources to support their learning, as well as supported occasions to practice, understand, and expand on their identities as bilingual individuals. Mr. Miller has adopted the translanguaging model to try to meet his students' needs. To be more specific about how Mr. Miller enacted translanguaging, we present a lesson he taught from a thematic unit on school bullying.

To prepare the lesson

On Monday, Mr. Miller asks the students during the week to do some thinking about or research the issue of school bullying. "You can talk with your parents, interview family members and friends, read books, search online, or watch YouTube videos on school bullying issues. You should take notes in the language of your choice to record your research and thinking, and then bring your notes to share in class next Monday."

During the lesson

When the students come to class on the following Monday, they share their notes in groups. Some share the stories they read about in novels or online blogs and news stories. Some share the experiences they learned about through talking to their parents and others, or how they encountered bullying situations in their own lives in and out of school. They switch back and forth between their home languages and English depending on their audience or what they are talking about, with speakers and listeners making sure that everyone understands the conversation.

A few minutes later, Mr. Miller gets the class together and reads aloud a picture book on school bullying. The book, *Say Something* by Peggy Moss and Lea Lyon (2004) is narrated from a young student's perspective: She witnesses others being mean to her peers and learns that being a silent bystander is not the solution.

Mr. Miller reads the book in English and shows the pictures to the class, without stopping the first time. During a second reading, he reads a section and then pauses, letting students turn and talk to their desk mates, to discuss what they have learned and what they are thinking. They can speak in any language in their small-group discussion.

When the second read-aloud and discussion are completed, Mr. Miller writes key words related to bullying in English on the board, and invites students to add different home language words under the English words. If they don't know how to write the words in their home language, they can check the words online or in dictionaries (of their home languages) on the bookshelf. Phonemic spelling of the words using the Latin (English) alphabet is also acceptable.

Then Mr. Miller asks the students to write, for 2–3 minutes in any language, their thoughts about the book and connections between the story and their prior research. After this individual quick-write, students get into collaborative groups: Some groups include students who speak the same home language, most groups have English-only students, and one group has students with diverse language backgrounds. Some of the groups have five to six members, whereas others are as small as two to three people. Different languages are used in the group discussions, and students are comfortably translanguaging from home language to English and vice versa. When the teacher arrives at a group with a language he doesn't know, the students immediately shift their language to English so the teacher can understand them.

After 5–7 minutes of group discussion, Mr. Miller asks each group to create a list of questions about bullying they want to investigate. One or 2 minutes later, each group presents their questions to the class. Most questions are in English, though some questions include words in other languages. Mr. Miller records the questions on the board in English, and also includes in parentheses some of the significant non-English vocabulary used by students. The teacher and the students go over the list of questions posed by the groups, and choose four questions on school bullying that students want to explore further:

1. How can we work together to fight against bullying in our school?
2. What should we do when we encounter bullying behaviors?
3. What kind of people tend to bully others?
4. What kind of people usually get bullied?

The students are grouped together based on the questions they chose for the next step in the unit. Before the end of the class, the new groups work together to plan how they would find out information to respond to their chosen questions. They are to do some prep work at home and continue their research at school the next day. Mr. Miller concludes the class with the following statement:

> In the next couple of days, you will work as a group to dig deeper and find more information about the question you selected. Before our next class, try to find some resources that can help you in your task. These could be books, digital texts, videos, or people. Your resources can be in any language you want, but please share your information tomorrow in English so we can all understand you.

In this translanguaging class, students are engaging with multimodal and multilingual literacies, reading content-based texts in print and online in multiple languages, as well as listening and watching multilingual videos. In addition, there are multilingual resources in the classroom, including dictionaries, glossaries, and classroom computers for digital translations. Many students speak more languages than the teacher. In this classroom, students often take the lead to facilitate learning in their home languages and to use translanguaging to support themselves and others.

The teacher in this classroom does not defer the responsibility of building his students' English skills to the ESL or bilingual teachers, nor does he adopt an English-only approach, as is common in regular education classrooms. Instead, he purposefully makes this classroom a multilingual learning environment that includes all students. As pointed out earlier, with help from the students, parents, and community members, this teacher has his everyday learning objectives, classroom rules, and assignment guidelines written in multiple languages, and also has a word wall that includes key vocabulary written in different languages. Students play a critical role in making this multilingual environment possible: They take on translation duties whenever needed and help one another in group discussions or projects. With effective communication as a key goal, these citizens of the 21st century support all participants so no speaker is silenced and no listener is sidelined. Indeed, with a focus on equity and social justice, the class has often talked about how overt and subtle behaviors can marginalize or empower different groups or individuals. Because of that, students can often be heard inviting quiet students into conversations, asking how things are said in different languages, and checking for understanding before moving on.

Mr. Miller groups the students based on their needs: Sometimes students sharing a language are grouped together so they can discuss their work in their native language; sometimes EBs are grouped with peers who do not speak their home language so they can practice using English with their peers. In addition, while his English-proficient students are working independently or in collaborative groups, Mr. Miller often spends time working with the EBs as a group to give these students extra help and minilessons in support of their content and language learning.

In this translanguaging classroom, though English is more dominant than it would be in a bilingual classroom, the students can use any language(s) of their choice in reading, writing, and group discussions. Even though the majority of students in this class use English most of the time, choosing to use another language in reading, group discussions, writing, or even responding to the teacher's questions in class are welcomed practices; the class works together to translate and make sense of the contribution. Students who do so are not looked down upon or excluded, but are rather given support and earn the admiration of their peers. Their bilingual and biliteracy competence is valued and highly respected in this community.

The classroom library has bilingual books and books in different languages. During reading workshop time, students can read books of their choice in English or their home languages, or books they brought from home or that are available to them online. They also can write their reading response in any language they choose. Mr. Miller tries to meet with all students individually once or twice a week to confer with them about their reading. Students talk about their books with the teacher in English, but if they feel too challenged, they can have a peer support them as a translator. Most students value their individual time with the teacher and try hard to speak English. The newcomers do need their peers' help when conferencing with their teacher. Through these individual conferences, Mr. Miller not only becomes familiar with each student and his or her reading progress, but also learns about different books, especially those written in the students' native languages. In addition, Mr. Miller also gets to add to his own language repertoire by learning key vocabulary in his students' home languages and incorporating it in conversations with the students and in his teaching.

In this school, pull-out and push-in ESL services are combined to serve the students identified as English learners. The ESL teacher comes to the mainstream class to meet her students once a week so she can get to know the classroom two to three times a week for special instruction. When she pushes in, she often has discussions with the EB students about the books they read, or works with them in producing English translations of their work. Through the translation process, students learn different ways of expressing themselves and gain opportunities to note and discuss the similarities and differences of language rules between English and their native languages, gaining met-alinguistic insight. When the students go to the ESL classroom, they often take their books with them to have reading discussions there or to work on their English translations in the ESL room with the help of the ESL teacher. In this way, rather than having different curricula with different teachers or in different rooms, the EBs can continue with their learning between the two environments with extra support from ESL service.

Since Mr. Miller adopted a translanguaging approach in his teaching, he found not only his EB students' becoming more engaged in their learning, but also that all the students in his class seemed to enjoy learning with and from the EB students about their languages, their perspectives, and the differences in different languages. As he said,

> None of the students are bothered by the languages spoken around them that they don't understand, which had been a major concern when I first embarked on this journey. Instead, they have fun listening, imitating, and even teaching me how to say some languages right. It is their engagement in learning in this multilingual community that convinced me of the effectiveness of this approach and makes me want to do more for all my students.

Unfortunately, in comparison to bilingual and ESL classrooms, we have found only a few mainstream classroom teachers like Mr. Miller, who are fully committed to adopting a translanguaging approach in their rooms. We suspect that this discrepancy is due to differences in experience with and knowledge of bilingualism and bilingual pedagogy. ESL and bilingual teachers have professional expertise and firsthand experience in working with emergent bilinguals, and many of them are bilinguals themselves. As such, they are much more likely to have encountered translanguaging pedagogy in their professional development activities and, because of their background knowledge and experience, they are also more likely to recognize its potential and feel comfortable enough to try it out in their teaching. On the other hand, mainstream teachers often report feeling underprepared to work with emergent bilinguals (Calderón et al., 2011).

Given this, even if they do come across translanguaging ideas, they may not feel knowledgeable or confident enough to bring it into their classrooms. Adopting a translanguaging curriculum not only requires teachers to enact a paradigm shift in teaching beliefs and practice, but it also demands additional effort in lesson planning, resource searching, and community building. To do so, mainstream teachers need to see beyond the single-minded focus of our monolingually oriented education system and develop special care, empathy, and sensitivity for EBs who are often marginalized linguistically and socially in school for being different. Then they will see their differences as valuable instructional resources rather than as deficits to be remediated. For mainstream classroom teachers, the shift from "English-only" to a multilingual perspective in their teaching practice requires a fundamental thinking shift in their teaching beliefs and in how they value and embrace all their students. As Mr. Miller expressed it:

> It is easy to say: We should value all our students' languages, their funds of knowledge, but to truly put this into our practice, and figure out how to make it really benefit all the students, it takes a lot of thinking, planning, and even soul searching. I even asked myself at the beginning: Is it worthwhile to put forth so much effort just for a few EB students in my class? Now I found the more translanguaging strategies I tried in my teaching, the more engaged all my students are in their learning. I also realized that translanguaging teaching is not just engaging all my students in learning language and school subjects, but it also makes them grow as good citizens for a democratic society. In this multilingual community, I am growing together with my students. I love it!

Mr. Miller has said it well: Translanguaging teaching is more than just engaging EB students in their learning; it also cultivates good citizenship habits in all our students for a democratic society. As teachers, we need to re-examine our practice and constantly search for new ways of teaching to make our classroom more open and democratic, where we can grow together with our students to become better citizens for our multilingual and multicultural world.

CONCLUSION

In this chapter, we have presented challenges faced by schools with increasing numbers of emergent bilingual students. These challenges include a shortage of qualified bilingual and ESL teachers, underprepared mainstream teachers, and limited resources to serve emergent bilingual students. These problems are compounded by high demands for accountability that require all students to meet grade-level curriculum standards regardless of their language and learning backgrounds or time spent in U.S. schools. In contrast, we have presented translanguaging school and classroom portraits to illustrate how teachers can use translanguaging teaching models not only to respond to school challenges, but also to maximize students' learning potentials, engaging all students in content and language learning no matter what their backgrounds or how long they have been in U.S. schools. Translanguaging is not a program, but a model that can be practiced with emergent bilingual students in any learning setting—ESL, bilingual, or mainstream ELA classrooms and even content courses. In translanguaging classrooms, teachers do not need to know all the students' languages, but they do need to do the following:

- Provide space and resources, and help students learn and work with one another, becoming co-learners rather than sole knowledge givers or language teachers
- Engage students by creating a multilingual learning environment to maximize all students' learning potentials and engage all students in active participation in reading, speaking, and writing activities (being authors, translators, and interpreters)
- Identify, respect, and highlight students' expertise and background knowledge, letting them play important roles in teaching about their cultures and their languages and helping them learn new knowledge, new languages, and new worlds
- Invite parents and other members of the students' communities into the classroom to be guest speakers or demonstrate their knowledge and expertise by participating in school and class projects, so that they are part of the children's school learning

In translanguaging classrooms, students, as well as their families and communities, are both resources and agents in their education while teachers are co-learners with students in their learning community. Together they journey as global citizens through translanguaging, and in so doing, they enrich and transform their classroom and school community.

CHAPTER 5

Translanguaging in Action

In the previous chapters we have discussed the academic and social challenges for emergent bilingual students in a variety of educational and social settings, and have illustrated common challenges faced by schools as they work to serve the needs of their linguistically diverse students. To address these challenges, we have shown how enacting translanguaging practice in these very same diverse settings can offer promising solutions. In this chapter we offer some practical recommendations for implementing translanguaging strategies in different educational contexts and respond to some common questions raised by teachers regarding translanguaging in practice.

At the outset, we want to emphasize that translanguaging is not a program, but a pedagogical model grounded on pluralist theory. It can be used in any settings with emergent and experienced bilingual students. There are three key tenets for translanguaging practice, each of which we will review below:

- Individuals have a single, unified linguistic repertoire.
- Teachers are co-learners in their classrooms.
- Translanguaging practice is purposefully and systematically incorporated in both instructional planning and practice.

First, we want to stress the fundamental principle of the translanguaging model: Regardless of how many languages they speak, individuals have a single, unified linguistic repertoire, which cannot be forcibly separated in thinking, communicating, and learning. Given this, all languages of the students in the learning community have significant roles to play in supporting their learning and their development into accomplished bi/multilinguals. Only when teachers hold this belief in educating EB students can they fully understand translanguaging theory and practice.

Second, teachers need to see themselves as co-learners in their classrooms, willing to learn from students, their languages, and their cultures, rather than functioning as the sole possessors of knowledge, "the experts," or the only language instructors in classrooms. Rather, teachers need to highlight students' unique expertise and background knowledge, let them play an active and empowered role in sharing their cultures and languages, and help them enter and move into new knowledge, a new language, and a new world. Students, along with their families and community members, are collaborators, participants, and experts regarding various topics in this learning community.

Third, teachers need to systematically and purposefully design lessons to create spaces for translanguaging practice: Students can choose to read, respond, discuss in small groups, and draft in any languages, while the teacher reads, responds, recasts, explains, and communicates in English or any other target language. Teachers don't need to know all the students' languages, but do need to provide space and resources, and help students learn and work with one another. In a translanguaging classroom, students have access to bi/multilingual books, reading materials, word walls, pictures, dictionaries, and online translation programs. Lesson objectives, key vocabulary and phrases, essential questions, study guides, and group discussion questions should be bi/multilingual. Multilingual displays in the school should be aligned with lesson units and the curriculum. Students, bi/multilingual adults in the building, family/community members, and technologies are all translation resources. It takes communal effort to create rich multilingual schools and classrooms.

In the following, we offer specific suggestions for using translanguaging strategies in different learning settings for EB students. Many strategies can be used across all learning settings. We also address common issues and questions that teachers raise regarding suggestions we make for translanguaging classrooms.

IN BILINGUAL EDUCATION SETTINGS

Most bilingual programs in U.S. schools are considered transitional—beginning EB students are to study subject-area content in their native language while developing their English language skills. In many European countries this kind of program is known as "mother tongue instruction" (Ganuza & Hedman, 2017). In such settings students' home language is purposefully included in their education only until students reach proficiency in the target language. In translanguaging bilingual classrooms, students should not be limited to only using their native language, but should be given choices to read, draft, and discuss in any languages, without being limited to a single language assigned to each time block or subject.

It is important to remember that even students who share a language may be very diverse in terms of other language varieties they may know, in educational experiences, and literacy levels in their common heritage language, as well as in oral proficiency and literacy in the majority language. Students with interrupted formal education in their home countries may not have had enough first language literacy to readily learn content-area knowledge simply by being given access to written material in their home language. In addition, as shown through examples in Chapter 4, it is not uncommon to have in a bilingual program some students who have different home languages from the majority of the class. The benefit of giving students language choice in their learning is that they are not confined to one level, one language proficiency, or the same learning pace, but all students can make progress at their own pace, differentiated for optimal learning potential.

Now we want to respond to four questions teachers in bilingual settings often ask us about implementing translanguaging.

How do I find books written in different languages on the same topics and at different levels? This is a common question from bilingual teachers who want to adopt a translanguaging model in their instruction. Indeed, this is a practically insurmountable hurdle if you are only searching for textbooks or print books on specific subjects. However, the pool of learning resources available broadens significantly when you expand your search to include various types of materials in the students' home languages and the school's target language(s) such as the following:

- Print and digital textbooks
- Picture books and other trade books in print and digital formats
- Websites
- Online videos on YouTube and other online platforms
- Podcasts and other audio recordings

Content knowledge is the main objective for bilingual programs, and therefore, as long as students can engage in vigorous learning of the content knowledge aligned with your curriculum goals, they should be encouraged to read (or watch or listen) to learn in any languages and modalities.

In fact, we recommend that identifying diverse materials to support student learning should not be the exclusive responsibility (and privilege) of the teacher. Rather, you should guide students in how to search for reading materials on certain topics at their appropriate levels, through credible and trustworthy sources, and create plentiful supported opportunities for them to do so. Beyond alleviating your burden, this is a significant critical literacy practice that empowers students as uniquely qualified evaluators, information seekers, and selectors of texts and other resources.

How do I teach a subject topic to students who read different materials in different languages and formats? This is a good question. You don't need to read everything students are reading. You can teach in the language and materials of your choice, and the students can choose to read the selected reading materials or the materials on the same topic in the language and format they can better understand. This individualized reading builds the background for them to follow along with your lessons, participate in the group and class discussions, and lay a knowledge base for new content and academic vocabulary development. It is easier to teach a subject when students have background knowledge related to the subject, and lessons become more vibrant and informative when different members of the class can offer information and ideas from diverse sources. It is much easier to conduct group discussion when all students can bring some knowledge to the table. It can even give rise to valuable critical literacy discussions about the nature of knowledge and ways to judge the reliability of sources and to address issues of perspective.

How can I carry out group discussions when students are reading different materials and speak in different languages? Group discussions can be a challenge when students read different texts written in different languages and at different levels. In a translanguaging classroom students should be grouped based on their specific needs and learning purposes, such as in the following ways:

- Peers who speak the same language when they want to discuss their reading/writing in their home language.
- Peers who read books in the same language (home or English) so they can discuss their reading in that language. They don't have to read the same books or materials, but they should have read about the same topic.
- Peers of mixed levels so they can learn and support one another (either in home language or English).
- Peers of mixed languages so they can practice English speaking and listening with a focus on effective communication.

As we discussed in Chapters 2 and 4, strategic grouping gives all students various opportunities to participate in class activities and discussion. You should make sure that the students have diverse learning opportunities by working with peers of different learning levels and backgrounds. We recommend that you sit with the groups that need your guidance the most. You may often have to rely on students to translate and help you contribute to group discussions.

How do I evaluate students' work if it is written in a language I don't understand? We believe the final work, either presentations to the class or written work submitted to the teacher, should be in a language that the majority of the class or the teacher can understand. After all, a significant characteristic in the real-life communications of experienced bilinguals is that they shape their contributions so that they can be understood by their audience. With the help of adults at home or in the school, peers in class, or technology programs, students can translate their work into English or publish their work in bi/multilingual formats. Both bilingual teachers and ESL teachers should work with the students to edit their translation and finalize their work, which is a great opportunity to teach language skills in a meaningful, authentic context.

IN ESL EDUCATION SETTINGS

The purpose of ESL education is to help students develop their English language skills. Commonly, an ESL class can have students at different English levels and with vastly varied home language contexts: Some may be newcomers who barely understand any English, and some may be labeled as long-term ELs who can speak English quite fluently but are struggling with English reading and writing. Even though language is the focus of ESL programs, it is hard to teach or learn a new language out of context. Students can get easily bored when they are drilled with language rules and conventions, which have little relevance to their learning in the regular classrooms. English-only policies or English-immersion practices are at the heart of traditional ESL instruction.

However, this traditional practice has kept many EB students silent for a long time, or has resulted in their slow development as readers, writers, and language learners. In order to engage all students at different stages of English learning into meaningful reading, writing, speaking, and language learning activities, ESL teachers need to let EBs discuss their reading, share their understanding, and draft their writing using all of their languages. Even though the development of EB students into accomplished users of English is still an important goal, teachers need to keep in mind that not all the language objectives for EBs are specific to English. Indeed, many fundamental literacy objectives, such as providing evidence to support interpretations, analyzing text structure, and evaluating the validity of arguments and reliability of sources, are not at all unique to English, and their exploration can and should engage all of students' languages and language knowledge. ESL teachers can recast, rephrase, and respond to EBs' words in English, which is a much more effective way to teach a new language. As García et al. (2017) emphasize, "translanguaging classrooms show us that bilingual students perform better with *targeted* language features when they have been given ample opportunities to perform tasks using the full features of their *entire* linguistic repertoires first" (p. 39).

How can I teach a common language lesson with a translanguaging approach? You can teach a lesson on a certain English language rule, in English of course, and then let students discuss and explain it to one another in a language with which they are more comfortable. Part of this discussion can be about how the particular language feature is used (if at all) in the students' heritage languages, thus allowing students to make explicit connections between English and other languages. In this way, EBs not only become metacognitively aware of similarities and differences among languages in their linguistic repertoire, but also students at different levels can help one another and even reteach the lesson on certain language rules to the students who need extra time and help in their learning. For instance, students can look into books written in English to identify how a certain rule is used (e.g., tense, possessive nouns, or plural forms), and for this activity students can use their home languages in their discussion, so everyone, no matter at what stage, can participate and be engaged in this language learning activity. Once all students are engaged in their learning, you are not the only teacher in the classroom. You can act as a facilitator to make sure EBs are making steady progress.

If I let students use their home language in my room, does that mean I don't give them maximum time or opportunity to practice English? This is a common concern among many ESL teachers, as they realize that most of their EB students barely have any chance to speak or use English in their regular classrooms (most of them keep silent) and that their time in their ESL class is often the only chance that these students get to speak up, read something at their level, or feel they are the focus of instruction. In response to this concern, we have to say that immersion of students in English doesn't necessarily mean immersion in learning. If they don't understand, they may simply tune out. If they can't participate, they are likely to lose interest and motivation in learning. If they can only learn basic language skills but are not able to engage in meaningful reading, writing, and discussion, they are likely to get bored and develop low self-esteem regarding their ability to learn English. In order to engage them, the learning has to be meaningful and intellectually challenging at their level. For EBs, their competence in English may not match their intellectual level, so you need to enable them to use the language(s) they know to maximize their learning potential.

Would some students choose the easy way out by using their home language (for speaking, reading, and writing) rather than pushing themselves to use English as much as they can in their learning? No doubt, there may be a few students like this, but our experience is that the majority of students really try their best to learn English once they are interested in learning and find learning meaningful. EBs know how important it is for them to develop English proficiency in this world that prioritizes English, for their current lives in and out of school, and for their future. They are very frustrated and even ashamed when they cannot make effective progress in English learning. Although in the translanguaging classroom there are many opportunities for students to choose which language they will use as they are pursuing learning activities, you should still have explicit English-specific objectives for your instruction. Students should not just use their home language to talk. They should use it to talk about the English language, to discuss texts they are reading (to build background knowledge, to explain their comprehension, or to review what has been read in English), and to outline or draft their writing so they can record and develop their ideas before they rewrite or translate their work into English. This process is one of the best ways to develop English grammar knowledge and vocabulary, and also to practice the writing process. Students use their home language for the purpose of expressing themselves as learners, connecting their language learning with their thinking and emotions, and as rehearsal for their English performance.

How long and how much should I let EB students use their home language? Is this only for beginning EBs? Once they have developed enough English proficiency, should I push them to use more English than their home language? Translanguaging gives choices and spaces for students to use any language to engage them and maximize their learning opportunity, but does not set rules, limits, or boundaries for EBs in their language choice for the purpose of their learning. After all, the objective is not simply to help them develop into proficient speakers of English who happen to know another language, but rather to help them grow into flexible, adaptive, accomplished bilinguals who have greater confidence in using language for communication. Experienced bilinguals constantly translanguage in their everyday lives and at work. The context, the audience, and the events (or topics) determine how and in what language they choose to read and to express themselves. If bilinguals are asked how much and how often they speak one language or the other, it would be hard for them to give a simple straightforward answer, since it all depends. The translanguaging model seeks to bring this norm into the classroom, and let students purposely choose languages they possess to reach their optimal learning potentials. Therefore, our response to your questions is this: You should share with your students the purpose of language choice and the goals of learning both content and language, and work with them through flexible use of any language in whichever medium as long as they aspire to reach their learning goals.

How can I as an ESL teacher work with regular classroom teachers within the translanguaging model? Your collaboration with regular classroom teachers would benefit EB students greatly, not only by helping them develop their English language ability but also by enabling them to study the grade-level curriculum along with their peers. As an ESL teacher, you probably are bilingual yourself and have firsthand experience with translanguaging practice, which is the reason why many ESL teachers have adopted the translanguaging model in their teaching. You can help inform other teachers and administrators in the building about the potential of translanguaging practice and coach colleagues in adopting the translanguaging model across your school. If the regular classroom teachers are committed to a translanguaging teaching model and allow the students to use their choice of language to develop content knowledge, it would a great help to them if you, as an ESL teacher, can assist with translations or teach students the English language they need to write their final report, work on their presentation, or edit their essays. Unfortunately, it is always challenging for both ESL teachers and regular classroom teachers to find time for such collaboration.

We are not suggesting that you should totally ignore your own ESL curriculum. Instead, you should teach the language skills and vocabulary the students need to study along with their English-proficient peers. This can be done in both pull-out and push-in ESL situations. In addition, you can help students search for reading materials and other resources online or at the library in different languages on the subject topics they are learning in regular classrooms, and provide them with time to read and discuss the materials when they are in your room or in their regular classrooms. This kind of work can help mainstream classroom teachers greatly in teaching EBs regardless of whether or not they practice translanguaging.

IN MAINSTREAM CLASSROOM SETTINGS

In mainstream classrooms across the United States, the number of EB students is rapidly increasing. Even though some of the bilingual students may have scored high enough on English language proficiency tests to no longer be deemed as needing ESL services, it is important to remember that they do not have the same English proficiency as their native English-speaking peers. These students, including those who still receive ESL services, are expected to learn the same academic materials as their peers, as well as continue to develop proficiency in English.

Regular classroom teachers are given the responsibility to teach language and content to EB students and ensure that they pass end-of-year assessments along with their English-proficient peers. However, research has consistently documented a large achievement gap between native English speakers and emergent bilinguals in the United States (e.g., Goldenberg, 2008).

To make sure that all EBs study the same content as their peers, they need to be allowed access to valid resources with information on the topics so they can attend to lessons, understand their peers, and participate in learning activities. These resources can be in a variety of formats (including audio and video) and in languages the students can understand. Otherwise, they will waste their time, waiting for when they can study at the same pace with their English-proficient peers, which may never happen in a system that does not wait for them to catch on. EBs need to be allowed to read and to discuss and draft in the languages of their choice. For English-only speaking teachers, this can be a challenge, which will be addressed below through a question-and-answer format.

How do I know what EBs are reading or how much they comprehend their reading when I don't understand what they read? Teachers can usually tell when students are engaged in their reading. In reading workshops where students can choose their own reading, you don't need to know everything your students are reading, as long as they are reading during the independent reading time. If you want to know what they are reading, you can join their group discussion or conduct a conference with the help of peers acting as student-translators. You can let these students compose their reading responses in drawings with brief captions or look at their translated work (with the help of translation software). Translanguaging teachers have learned to let go of some control in their classrooms, but to trust students and to teach them to take control of their own learning. The more limitations and control you put on teaching and learning, the more passive and the less engaged or motivated students become as learners.

How can I help these students' writing when I don't understand what they write? As teachers, you don't need to be able to read what students write for themselves, such as notes, outlines, or drafts. But when they are writing for final submission, for you to give your response or feedback, you do need to understand it. You need to allow EBs time for completing translations and to understand the translation process as a language teaching and learning process. This leads to building a metaperspective of how languages work to convey meaning, and allows students to gain awareness of and unpack their own language learning process. Emergent bilinguals are still developing their new language skills. They need time and instruction to learn and practice new language rules. Translation of their work involves using and learning language skills in a meaningful context. They can use electronic translation programs to do the first draft of the translation, which would give you a rough idea of the content, even though it may not be very accurate. From this rough draft, you can work with the students to make it as accurate as possible to the student-writers' intentions, and teach English language rules and writing conventions during this translation process. You may need help with the translation from more advanced EBs in your classroom, or you can collaborate with ESL teachers or other bilingual professionals in the building.

What should I do with newly arrived EB students when no one in the class shares their home language? It is understandable that these students would feel disoriented, bewildered, and lonely. You need to make extra effort to get to know the newcomers and to create supportive, inclusive structures. First of all, you want these students to feel that they are welcome and that their home language is valued in your room. Not only should they learn the majority language, English, but you also should learn about them, their experiences, and their language. Translanguaging is not just using multiple languages in your teaching and learning, but valuing all languages and seeing them all as learning resources. It is hard for these students to share their home language reading or writing with the class, but if they are allowed to read and write in their home language during the reading and writing time, they would feel that they are just like everyone else in this learning community. As the students begin to learn English, you can encourage and support them as they author bilingual texts and as they translanguage their way through home language resources. It is also important to purposefully pair them with other students who are patient and caring, and love to teach and help others, to accompany these students on their journey. Encourage them to help one another with their language learning, and also let them show you how they can learn one another's language. Of course, you need to find time to regularly work with these newcomers individually, and translate key questions and vocabulary related to the lessons, reading, writing, and homework requirements or classroom routines into their home language as well, with the help of technology, a foreign-language dictionary, people in the building, or community members.

How can I find time to help my EB students who have different home language backgrounds and are at different levels with their English, and even at different levels of their first language literacy, to make progress in both their content and language learning? This is perhaps the most challenging situation for your teaching, especially if you don't share your students' home and cultural backgrounds or their formal school experience. It is impossible for you to know the languages and cultures of all your students when they are so diverse. But we urge you to open your arms to embrace them all with pluralistic attitudes and an inclusive classroom culture. You should try your best to have multilingual and multicultural texts, with references and resources covering different topics and different languages in your class library. We encourage you to guide your students, with the help of their family members, to search for books and reading or learning materials in multiple languages, which are age appropriate, curriculum related, and at different levels (English or first language literacy).

Then you need to give students time and space in class to read, discuss, and draft their writing in their choice of languages. They may not read, speak, and write at the same level or proficiency either in their home language or English, but it is important that they can all participate in the same learning activities. As we suggested in the section on bilingual education settings, you need to group students differently for different purposes or learning goals, which not only gives students different learning opportunities with different peers in class, but also helps them get to know all their peers in the community rather than only those who share the same back-grounds. As the teacher, you do instruct—explaining the content, helping students develop the academic language associated with the content they are learning, and guiding them to do the research to expand their knowledge beyond merely what they have read and experienced.

Take advantage of the diversity in your classroom. To have students showcase their cultural heritage, you should share literature with the same themes and topics in different languages and traditions (such as folklores, fables, and fairytales), and present content knowledge with multicultural and multilingual perspectives (math, science, and social studies, such as with the Ishango bone in Chapter 3). Further, you can invite students' family members as guest speakers (on any topics of their expertise) and position the students as translators for guest speakers. You can also publish and show-case students' work in multiple languages.

Once you take on a facilitator's role and see yourself also as an emergent bilingual, rather than merely as an information supplier or language teacher in your classroom, your teaching job will be less challenging and overwhelming in your diverse classroom. We urge you to see every student in your learning community as a resource, an asset, and a co-teacher, where they all work together to learn, to grow, and to achieve, although all may not move at the same pace, learn in the same language, or take the same route to reach common goals. Classrooms today resemble the real world, where there are more multilinguals than monolinguals, and we all make contributions in our unique ways and with our individual talents and abilities.

TRANSLANGUAGING AND 21ST-CENTURY GLOBAL COMPETENCE

Dennis Van Roekel, the president of the National Education Association (NEA, 2010), stated:

> The 21st century isn't coming; it's already here. And our students have the opportunity and challenge of living and working in a diverse and rapidly chang-ing world. Public schools must prepare our young people to understand and address global issues, and educators must re-examine their teaching strategies and curriculum so that all students can thrive in this global and interdependent society. (p. 1)

This NEA policy brief points out that global competence refers to the ac-quisition of in-depth knowledge and understanding of international issues, an appreciation of and ability to learn and work with people from diverse linguistic and cultural backgrounds, proficiencies in a foreign language, and skills to function productively in an interdependent world community.

However, "most American students, low-income and minority groups in particular, lag behind their peers in other countries in their knowledge of world geography, foreign languages, and cultures" (p. 1).

According to the Census Bureau's data from the American Community Survey, one in five U.S. residents speaks a language other than English at home (Camarota, 2015). Many of those who speak a foreign language at home are U.S.-born; of the nearly 63.2 million foreign-language speakers, 44% (27.7 million) were born in the United States. And there are over 250 languages spoken among these foreign-language speakers. These are tremendously valuable human resources and precious national treasures. The United States can be very competitive globally if we are able to leverage these resources, not only to preserve them, but to continue to invest in their development. A translanguaging model not only enables EB students to maximize their learning potential, but also gives them space and opportunity to continue developing the proficiency of their home language in our classrooms so as to become proficient bilinguals with well-developed biliteracy skills. Such knowledgeable citizens with sophisticated and flexible communication skills can be a most valuable resource for U.S. society. In addition, translanguaging classrooms can be important training grounds for supporting young people's social development and honing their skills and their intellect as active, democratic citizens committed to making space for all voices to be heard and for transformative action for social justice. As noted by García et al. (2017), "by making space for students to language on their own terms and participate fully in academic conversations and work, we are modeling the kind of active participation needed for the creation of a more just world" (p. 14).

A translanguaging pedagogic model is not meant to benefit only emergent bilingual students, but to cultivate the development of all students' global competence by studying with and among diverse students. Each of our emergent bilingual students brings his or her cultural heritage, language, and talents into our classrooms. Monolingual pedagogical orientations suppress and often are blind to the potential of these rich resources in the classroom. Translanguaging allows all students to read, discuss, and study content knowledge not just in English but in various other languages.

By listening to different languages in their classrooms, by encountering different perspectives and worldviews, by unsilencing marginalized voices, and by helping EB peers learn to speak English and translate their words into English, monolingual English-speaking students are also expanding their views of the world, developing their awareness or sense of other languages and cultures, which in turn cultivates their interest, motivation, and ability to appreciate different languages and cultures. Only when children grow up with people of different languages and cultures around them, will they develop linguistic curiosity, appreciate cultural differences, open their minds to diverse worldviews, and gain an urge to learn new languages and learn about different cultures. In translanguaging learning communities, all students work together to develop their 21st-century global competence and become global citizens in this interconnected society.

In this interdependent context, we need to embrace rather than ostracize "others," be open to differences rather than build walls to partition us from "others," and enrich and expand our vision to appreciate and value all diversities. The translanguaging model transcends language and national borders, and transforms relationships between teaching and learning, and between teachers and students. Translanguaging sees language as action—something we do—rather than treating it as a structure that locks us into a certain group, a certain nation, and a certain way of speaking, viewing, and being. Translanguaging, grounded in cosmopolitanism, liberates us, connects nations and cultures, and embraces the world as a whole. Translanguaging is needed more than ever in our classrooms today to cultivate our children's minds with democratic values, a social justice outlook, and global competence for our 21st-century interdependent world.

References

Abedi, J. (2008). Classification system for English language learners: Issues and recommendations. *Educational Measurement: Issues and Practice, 27*(3), 17–31.

Ada, A. F., & Savadier, E. (2004). *I love Saturdays y domingos* (Reprint edition). New York, NY: Atheneum Books for Young Readers.

Anh, N. N. (2014). *Ticket to childhood*. New York, NY: Overlook Press.

Bandiera, O., Mohnen, M., Rasul, I., & Viarengo, M. (2018). Nation-building Through Compulsory Schooling during the Age of Mass Migration. *The Economic Journal*, 1–48. https://doi.org/10.1111/ecoj.12624

Blackledge, A., & Creese, A. (2010). *Multilingualism: A critical perspective*. London, United Kingdom: Continuum.

Calderón, M., Slavin, R., & Sánchez, M. (2011). Effective instruction for English learners. *The Future of Children, 21*(1), 103–127.

Camarota, S. A. (2011). A record-setting decade of immigration: 2000 to 2010. *Center for Immigration Studies* [Website]. Retrieved from cis.org/Report/RecordSetting-Decade-Immigration-20002010

Camarota, S. A. (2015). One in five U.S. residents speaks foreign language at home. *Center for Immigration Studies* [Website]. Retrieved from cis.org/Report/One-Five-US-Residents-Speaks-Foreign-Language-Home

Capps, R., Fix, M., Murray, J., Ost, J., Passel, J. S., & Herwantoro, S. (2005). *The new demography of America's schools: Immigration and the No Child Left Behind Act* (ED490924). Washington, DC: Urban Institute (NJ1). Retrieved from eric.ed.gov/?id=ED490924

Celic, C., & Seltzer, K. (2011). *Translanguaging: A CUNY–NYSIEB guide for educators*. New York, NY: CUNY–NYS Initiative on Emergent Bilinguals. Retrieved from www.nysieb.ws.gc.cuny.edu/files/2012/06/FINAL-Translanguaging-Guide-With-Cover-1.pdf

Collins, B., & Cioè-Peña, M. (2016). Declaring freedom: Translanguaging in the social studies classroom to understand complex texts. In O. García & T. Kleyn (Eds.), *Translanguaging with multilingual students: Learning from classroom moments* (pp. 119–139). New York, NY: Routledge.

Council of Europe, Language Policy Division. (2006). *Plurilingual education in Europe: 50 years of international co-operation*. Strasbourg, France: Language Policy Division. Retrieved from https://www.ecml.at/Portals/1/documents/CoE-documents/plurinlingaleducation_en.pdf?ver=2017-02-07-160535-763

Criscione, W. (2018, February 1). Idaho schools are struggling to keep up with an increase in English-language learners. *Inlander.* Retrieved from www.inlander. com/spokane/idaho-schools-are-struggling-to-keep-up-with-an-increase-in-english-language-learners/Content?oid=7870811

Cummins, J. (1979). Linguistic interdependence and the educational development of bilingual children. *Review of Education Research, 49*(2), 222–251.

Cummins, J. (1980). The cross-lingual dimensions of language proficiency: Implications for bilingual education and the optimal age issue. *TESOL Quarterly, 14*(2), 175–187. Retrieved from doi.org/10.2307/3586312

Cummins, J. (1981a). Age on arrival and immigrant second language learning in Canada: A reassessment. *Applied Linguistics, 2*(2), 132–149.

Cummins, J. (1981b). Empirical and theoretical underpinnings of bilingual education. *Journal of Education, 163*(1), 16–29.

de Jong, E. (2011). *Foundations for multilingualism in education: From principles to practice.* Philadelphia, PA: Caslon.

Dorros, A. (1997). *Abuela* (Reprint edition). Oxford, United Kingdom: Puffin Books.

Education Commission of the States. (2014). What ELL training, if any, is required of general classroom teachers? Retrieved from ecs.force.com/mbdata/mbquestNB2?rep=ELL1415

Fix, M., & Passel, J. S. (2003). *U.S. immigration: Trends and implications for schools.* Washington, DC: Urban Institute.

Forzani, E., & Leu, D. J. (2017). Multiple perspectives on literacy as it continuously changes: Reflections on opportunities and challenges when literacy is deictic. *Journal of Education, 197*(2), 19–24. Retrieved from doi.org/10.1177/002205741719700203

Fu, D. (1995). *My trouble is my English: Asian students and their American dreams.* Portsmouth, NH: Heinemann.

Fu, D. (2003). *An island of English: Teaching ESL in Chinatown.* Portsmouth, NH: Heinemann.

Fu, D. (2009). *Writing between languages: How English language learners make the transition to fluency.* Portsmouth, NH: Heinemann.

Fu, D., & Matoush, M. (2014). *Focus on literacy.* London, United Kingdom: Oxford University Press.

Ganuza, N., & Hedman, C. (2017). Ideology versus practice: Is there a space for pedagogical translanguaging in mother tongue instruction? In B. Paulsrud, J. Rosén, B. Straszer, & A. Wedin (Eds.), *New perspectives on translanguaging and education* (pp. 190–208). Bristol, United Kingdom: Multilingual Matters.

García, O. (2009). *Bilingual education in the 21st century: A global perspective.* Malden, MA: Wiley-Blackwell.

García, O. (2011). Theorizing translanguaging for educators. In C. Celic & K. Seltzer (Eds.), *Translanguaging: Cuny-Nysieb guide for educators* (pp. 1–6). New York, NY: CUNY-NYSIEB, The Graduate Center, The City University of New York.

García, O., Johnson, S., & Seltzer, K. (2017). *The translanguaging classroom: Leveraging student bilingualism for learning.* Philadelphia, PA: Caslon.

García, O., & Li, W. (2014). *Translanguaging: Language, bilingualism and education.* London, United Kingdom: Palgrave Macmillan.

Goldenberg, C. (2008, Summer). Teaching English language learners: What the research does—and does not—say. *American Educator, 32*(2), 8–23, 42–44.

Grosjean, F. (1989). Neurolinguists, beware! The bilingual is not two monolinguals in one person. *Brain and Language, 36*(1), 3–15.

Grosjean, F. (2010). *Bilingual life and reality.* Cambridge, MA: Harvard University Press.

Gunderson, L. (2007). *English-only instruction and immigrant students in secondary schools: A critical examination.* New York, NY: Routledge.

Hakuta, K. (2011). Educating language minority students and affirming their equal rights: Research and practical perspectives. *Educational Researcher, 40*(4), 163–174.

Hopkins, M., Thompson, K. D., Linquanti, R., Hakuta, K., & August, D. (2013). Fully accounting for English learner performance: A key issue in ESEA reauthorization. *Educational Researcher, 42*(2), 101–108.

Hornberger, N. H. (2003). *Continua of biliteracy: An ecological framework for educational policy, research, and practice in mulitingual settings.* Clevedon, United Kingdom: Multilingual Matters.

Hutchinson, M., & Hadjioannou, X. (2017). The morphing assessment terrain for English learners in US schools. *English Teaching: Practice and Critique, 16*(1), 110–126. Retrieved from doi.org/10.1108/ETPC-02-2016-0037

Hymes, D. (1974). *Foundations in sociolinguistics: An ethnographic approach.* Philadelphia, PA: University of Pennsylvania Press.

Kibler, A. K., Walqui, A., & Bunch, G. C. (2015). Transformational opportunities: Language and literacy instruction for English language learners in the Common Core era in the United States. *TESOL Journal, 6*(1), 9–35. Retrieved from doi.org/10.1002/tesj.133

Martiniello, M. (2008). Language and the performance of English-language learners in math word problems. *Harvard Educational Review, 78*(2), 333–368, 429.

McGraw-Hill Education. (2017). *2017 English learner (EL) education report.* Retrieved from www.mheducation.com/prek-12/explore/2017-el-survey.html

Menken, K., Hudson, T., & Leung, C. (2014). Symposium: Language assessment in standards-based education reform. *TESOL Quarterly, 48*(3), 586–614. Retrieved from doi.org/10.1002/tesq.180

Mitchell. C. (2018, January 25). The national shortage of ELL teachers has caught the eye of Congress [Blog post]. *Education Week.* Retrieved from blogs.edweek.org/edweek/learning-the-language/2018/01/solve_ell_teacher_shortage.html

Moss, P., & Lyon, L. (2004). *Say something.* Thomaston, ME: Tilbury House.

National Center for Education Statistics (NCES). (2015). Common Core of Data (CCD). Retrieved from http://nces.ed.gov/ccd/tables/ACGR_RE_and_characteristics_2013-14.asp

National Center for Education Statistics (NCES). (2017). The condition of education 2017 (2017-144), English language learners in public schools. Retrieved from https://nces.ed.gov/programs/coe/indicator_cgf.asp

National Education Association (NEA). (2010). *Global competence is a 21st century imperative.* NEA Policy Brief. Retrieved from multilingual.madison.k12.wi.us/files/esl/NEA-Global-Competence-Brief.pdf

National Education Association (NEA). (2015). *Understanding the gaps: Who are we leaving behind—and how far?* Retrieved from www.nea.org/assets/docs/18021-Closing_Achve_Gap_backgrndr_7-FINAL.pdf

Olsen, L. (2014). *Meeting the unique needs of long tem English language learners: A guide for educators.* Washington, DC: National Education Association (NEA). Retrieved from www.ctdev.changeagentsproductions.org/wp-content/uploads/2015/04/LongTermEngLangLearner-NEA.pdf

Pavlenko, A. (2002). We have room for but one language here: Language and national identity in the US at the turn of the 20th century. *Multilingua: Journal of Cross-Cultural and Interlanguage Communication, 21*(2–3), 163–196. Retrieved from doi.org/10.1515/mult.2002.008

Plough, B., & Garcia, R. (2015). Whole school English learner reform: A heuristic approach to professional learning in middle schools. *Planning and Changing, 46*(1–2), 21–41.

Public Broadcasting System. (2001). Chinese Exclusion Treaty, 1880. Retrieved from www.pbs.org/weta/thewest/resources/archives/seven/chinxact.htm

Riordan, R. (2015). *The sword of summer.* Los Angeles, CA: Disney-Hyperion.

Roberts, C. A. (1995). Bilingual education program models: A framework for understanding. *Bilingual Research Journal, 19*(3–4), 369–378.

Rong, X. L., & Preissle, J. (2015). *Educating immigrant students in the 21st century: What educators need to know.* Thousand Oaks, CA: Sage.

Rory, J. L. (2012). *Education and social change: Contours in the history of American schooling.* New York, NY: Routledge.

Ryan, C. (2013). Language use in the United States: 2011. *American Community Service Reports, 22*, 1–16.

Sanatullova-Allison, E., & Robison-Young, V. A. (2016). Overrepresentation: An overview of the issues surrounding the identification of English language learners with learning disabilities. *International Journal of Special Education, 31*(2). Retrieved from eric.ed.gov/?id=EJ1111073

Schissel, J. L. (2014). Classroom use of test accommodations: Issues of access, equity, and conflation. *Current Issues in Language Planning, 15*(3), 282–295.

Sheng, Z., Sheng, Y., & Anderson, C. J. (2011). Dropping out of school among ELL students: Implications to schools and teacher education. *Clearing House, 84*(3), 98–103. Retrieved from doi.org/10.1080/00098655.2010.538755

Snyder, T. D., & Dillow, S. A. (2013). *Digest of education statistics, 2012* (NCES 2014–2015). [Appendix A: Guide to sources; Appendix B: Definitions; Appendix C: Index of table numbers]. Washington, DC: National Center for Education Statistics. Retrieved from eric.ed.gov/?id=ED544579

Sullivan, A. L. (2011). Disproportionality in special education identification and placement of English language learners. *Exceptional Children, 77*(3), 317–334.

Thomas, W. P., & Collier, V. (2002). *A national study of school effectiveness for language minority students long term academic achievement.* Santa Cruz, CA: Center for Research on Education, Diversity & Excellence.

U.S. Census Bureau. (2015, November 3). Census Bureau reports at least 350 languages spoken in U.S. homes (Press Release No. CB15-185). Retrieved from www.census.gov/newsroom/press-releases/2015/cb15-185.html

Wasem, R. E. (2013). *U.S. immigration policy: Chart book of key trends.* Washington, DC: Congressional Research Service.

WIDA Consortium. (2018). *ACCESS for ELLs 2.0 Interpretive Guide for Score Reports.* Madison, WI: Board of Regents of the University of Wisconsin System on behalf of the WIDA Consortium. Retrieved from https://wida.wisc.edu/sites/default/files/resource/Interpretive-Guide.pdf

Zaidi, R., & Rowsell, J. (2017). *Literacy lives in transcultural times.* New York, NY: Routledge.

Index

Abedi, J., 20
Abuela (Dorros), 48
Academic challenges
  among EBs, 9–11, 17–22
  among ELs, 31–51
  pull-out ESL programs and, 9
Academic language
  development of, time taken, 10
  interpersonal language vs., 35
Academic potential, maximizing,
  10–11
Academic trajectories, of ELs,
  18–19
ACCESS for ELLs 2.0 ELP test,
  20–21
Achievement gap, 31
Ada, A. F., 48
Age-appropriate reading materials,
  19
Alienation, in monolingual school
  setting, 60–61
American Community Survey, 110
"American ethnicity," 15
Americanization movement,
  English-centered, 15–16, 17
An Island of English (Fu), 4
Anderson, C. J., 20
Anh, N. N., 59
Arab immigrants, 16
Asian immigrants, 16
Assimilation. *See* Linguistic
  assimilation
August, D., 88

Bakhtin, Mikhail, x
Bandiera, Oriana, 15
Barnard, Henry, 15
Basic Interpersonal Communication
Skills (BICS), 35
Bicultural/Biculturalism
  author as, 8
  in early U.S., 15
Bilingual classrooms. *See also*
  Bilingual programs
  management issues, 78–79
  social studies class example,
    81–85
  translanguaging model/strategies
    in, 83–84, 100–103
Bilingual communities
  families/parents as school
    resource, 81, 85, 90
  translanguaging norm in, 6
*Bilingual Education in the 21st
  Century* (García), 6
Bilingual pedagogy, 83, 96
Bilingual practice
  language separation incompatible
    with, 45–47
  realities of, 48–49
Bilingual programs
  books for, 101
  concerns about, 44–47
  curriculum/language integration
    in, 4–5
  dual language. *See* Dual language
    bilingual programs
  privileging of English in, 47
  stigma attached to, 4, 9, 59, 60
  transitional. *See* Transitional
    bilingual programs
Bilingual teachers, 10, 41
  categorization by language
    proficiency, 78
  overseas recruitment of, 78
  shortage of, 75, 76–79

About the Authors

Danling Fu is a literacy professor in the College of Education, University of Florida, where she teaches courses on language arts methods and seminars on literacy/culture and composition theory/practice. She has worked with ESL and bilingual teachers and in the past 2 decades has conducted research on emergent bilingual students in New York City schools populated with new immigrants.

Xenia Hadjioannou is a language and literacy education professor at Pennsylvania State University's Harrisburg campus. She has worked with inservice and preservice teachers on teaching diverse students, including emergent bilinguals, and has helped administer professional development programs funded by the Office of English Language Acquisition, U.S. Department of Education.

Xiaodi Zhou is a language and literacy education professor in the College of Education of Georgia Southwestern State University. He has taught English in and out of the United States and conducted research on Mexican American youths in low-income communities. He writes English reading series and works on English writing textbooks for K–12 students in English as a foreign language (EFL) contexts.